Praise for

Still Wrestling

"This book is the best case study I know of to show that the meaning of a biblical text, to some large extent, depends on what we bring to the text. Ferguson brings to the text the gifts of his gut—the loss, anger, anguish, longing, and doubt—plus writing craftsmanship, imagination, humor, and honesty. The outcome for us is a fresh, rich study of the Bible that will connect with the deepest parts of our own guts. These texts will never sound the same. I am filled with gratitude for this book!"

> —Walter Brueggemann, Columbia Theological Seminary

"What an incredible opportunity we all have to grow from the life of Les Ferguson! There is no better guide to dealing with the doubts and questions that come from life's tragedies than Les. Follow his ongoing journey of insight and understanding in *Still Wrestling*."

> —Al Robertson, author and speaker from A&E's *Duck Dynasty*

"How can you hear hope in the stories of the Bible when you've experienced deep tragedy? *Still Wrestling* offers a path, but it is not an easy one. In a down-to-earth style, Les invites us into his world to see how he emerged from darkness, though his journey is not over yet. Les is still wrestling, as are we all."

> —John Mark Hicks, Professor of Theology, Lipscomb University

"I'm on my knees praying that you will let this powerful book change your life. This story is real. Les Ferguson is real. Pain and death are real. Heaven and victory are real! Walk with Les on this incredible journey—you'll be glad you did."

> —Ray Fulenwider, minister, Midlothian Church of Christ,
> author of *The Prayer-Driven Church*

"Les Ferguson tackles difficult questions of faith through the lens of his own brokenness and from the perspectives of biblical characters who also fell into the abyss. Yet, *Still Wrestling* is hopeful and faith-affirming. If you're seeking easy answers, you won't find them here. If you want to experience anew the grace that reaches into the deepest pit, read on."

> —Dr. David Enyart, retired Professor of Preaching, Johnson University

D1557402

"As a life-long member of the Church of Christ, I really admire my brother Les Ferguson's writing and his grappling with serious issues. I've done my own wrestling, and I truly appreciate his story."

—Pat Boone, entertainer, member of the Gospel Music Hall of Fame

"Les Ferguson's story is not a happy, trust Jesus and your life will always be sunshine and roses kind of story. It's a story of heartbreak and betrayal, of sleepless nights and more tears than anyone could count. It's also the story of a man who wrestles with God and lives to tell about it. Do yourself a favor and read this book."

—John Alan Turner, author of *Still Me: Life as a Work in Progress*

"How refreshing it is to read a book by a leader who doesn't ignore the hard questions. Les not only asks the questions, but he is honest enough to admit that there are times when it is difficult to speak with confidence about the presence of God. With refreshing candor, Les shows that suffering is not evidence that God is not with us. It is proof that he is."

—Gordon Dasher, elder, Whites Ferry Road Church of Christ

"Les tells his story without any sugar coating or false religiosity. It's a story of pain, but more than that, it's a story of overcoming. You'll find strength in this book. You may even find God in a way you never thought possible."

—Joe Beam, PhD, author of *Seeing the Unseen*

"I've known Les for years—before, during, and after the tragic events that took his wife and son. I've watched him wrestle with God and, against all odds, return to faith. This book will reach the hearts of the hurting. It is a necessary corrective to the smiling image we tend to show the world."

—Patrick Mead, minister, Fourth Avenue Church of Christ

"In *Still Wrestling*, Les allows us to share his experience of horror, anger, fear, and desperation, and he leads us to a deeper, more radical understanding of what it means to walk with God—a walk that takes us through, not around, the valley of the shadow of death."

—Bobby Valentine, minister, Eastside Church of Christ

"Preachers are taught to remind themselves that 'There are troubles and heartaches on every pew.' Most people who read this book will have experienced pain and loss. Those who haven't probably will. *Still Wrestling* will fortify you for whatever tragedy and loss come your way."

—Cecil May Jr., Dean Emeritus, Faulkner University

Still
Wrestling

Still Wrestling

FAITH RENEWED
THROUGH BROKENNESS

Les Ferguson Jr.

LEAFWOOD
PUBLISHERS
an imprint of Abilene Christian University Press

[handwritten inscription: Tonya, thanks for all the blessings you have sent over the years! Love & Peace! Les Ferguson]

STILL WRESTLING
Faith Renewed through Brokenness

LEAFWOOD
P U B L I S H E R S
an imprint of Abilene Christian University Press

LIBRARY OF CONGRESS CATALOGING-IN-PUBLICATION DATA
Names: Ferguson, Les, 1962- author.
Title: Still wrestling : faith renewed through brokenness / Les Ferguson Jr.
Description: Abilene : Leafwood Publishers, 2018.
Identifiers: LCCN 2017055694 | ISBN 9781684260508 (pbk.)
Subjects: LCSH: Ferguson, Les, 1962- | Christian biography. | Faith. |
    Consolation. | Suffering—Religious aspects—Christianity.
Classification: LCC BR1725.F47 A3 2018 | DDC 277.3/083092 [B] —dc23
LC record available at https://lccn.loc.gov/ 2017055694

Back cover photo courtesy of Aynsley Gibson Photography

Cover design by Bruce Gore | Gore Studios, Inc.
Interior text design by Sandy Armstrong, Strong Design

Leafwood Publishers is an imprint of Abilene Christian University Press
ACU Box 29138
Abilene, Texas 79699

1-877-816-4455
www.leafwoodpublishers.com

18 19 20 21 22 23 / 7 6 5 4 3 2 1

This book is tenderly dedicated to the life and memories of Karen and Cole. You are loved and missed by many.

Contents

Acknowledgments

This book you hold in your hands is a small part of my journey. Like maps of old that said "here be monsters," you are holding monstrous stories of pain. In contrast, you will also find stories of recovery and joy. But more so, within this book is the story of faith relearned. It is the story of learning to read the Bible far differently than I had ever read it before. And this has changed my relationship with God in dramatic ways.

You'll see that I've been wrestling with God. You may be tempted to think, "What's the big deal?" And the answer is, it's the biggest deal ever. If I could put it in perspective, imagine a five-year-old boy trying to manhandle the Hulk. Or, if wrestling is not your style, try to envision a novice bantamweight boxer going up against the heavyweight champion of the world. Wrestling or striving with God ripped the scab off the illusion that I ever was in control of my life.

Using a different metaphor, the storms have simply blown me into uncharted waters. I've had to face the fact I've been wholly inadequate at even standing on my own two feet. In that vein, while Isaiah talks about our own righteousness as being filthy rags before the Lord, my lightbulb moment has shown the futility of all my pride in accomplishment and place in life.

I hope you'll find my story uplifting. In the process of telling it, I've had a lot of people come alongside me as I've worked on this project. Besides all the good people from Leafwood Publishers (and Tom Williams too), there are many to be thankful for:

Thank you to my wife, Becki, for walking this road with me. Yours is a strength I could have never done without. I am blessed. You are a blessing. Proverbs 31 could easily be written of you.

Thank you to all our children. That you have blended together so well is a testimony to your own strength of character.

I don't know what I would have done without my own parents and siblings. You were strong for me when I was completely adrift.

Thank you to all my family—both old and new.

Thank you to all my friends. I am so grateful you never shied away from the magnitude of my pain.

And then there is the Lake Harbour Drive Church of Christ. I cannot adequately express my gratitude. You took a broken, timid, uncertain man and gave him a chance to do ministry and preaching again. It could have gone very badly. That it didn't is a testimony to the power, mercy, patience, and grace of both God and you.

Thank you, God. I don't know how to say it any better than with these simple words. Thank *You*, God.

You see, at just the right time, when we were still power-less, Christ died for the ungodly. Very rarely will anyone die for a righteous person, though for a good person someone might possibly dare to die. But God demonstrates his own love for us in this: While we were still sinners, Christ died for us.

Since we have now been justified by his blood, how much more shall we be saved from God's wrath through him! For if, while we were God's enemies, we were reconciled to him through the death of his Son, how much more, having been reconciled, shall we be saved through his life! Not only is this so, but we also boast in God through our Lord Jesus Christ, through whom we have now received reconciliation. (Rom. 5:6–11)

This then is my story. I pray it will be both a blessing and an encouragement.

I AM A MESS

I am a mess. Or, as they like to say here in the Deep South, a *hot* mess. The truth of the matter is I have always been a mess and that will never completely change, at least not on this side of eternity.

For years, I masqueraded as a successful husband, father, and preacher. In public, my family looked normal, functional, healthy, happy, and well. My career as a minister saw far more victories than defeats. The churches where I worked experienced growth spiritually and numerically. With the support and help of my family and church family, lives were changed, comfort was given, and hope was restored in numbers I will never be aware of.

But, can you say *dysfunctional*? If there was ever a word I disliked more than "retarded" (that word will be important later), it would most likely be "dysfunctional."

Understand this: I think everybody is dysfunctional. Can you remember the last time you said something to your spouse, kid, parent, friend, or to anybody else that you wished you could take back immediately? Can you remember the last time you didn't handle a situation well? Or the last time your expectations of someone else were way out of line with the reality of life and the flaws of others? Can you remember when you took out your frustrations and disappointments on people you loved, even though the immediate problem was no fault of theirs at all?

You, my friend, are guilty of impaired or abnormal functioning in whatever little social group you inhabit. You are ... drumroll, please ... dysfunctional. Or, as I like to say it, a mess. Maybe even a hot mess.

Sometimes our messes are quite hysterical. But no matter how humorous we make it out to be, dysfunctional has never been in God's plan for how we live our lives.

So, yes, I am a mess. Sometimes a big stinking mess, but I am not alone in my messiness. Not by a long shot. I have plenty of company in you too!

Still with me?

So back to my family and church family. Did I try to be the best I could? Most of the time, I gave it everything I had. But sometimes I got tired. Sometimes I was overwhelmed. Sometimes I stumbled well beyond my comfort zone. Sometimes I ventured way out of my league. And sometimes I walked on the ragged edge of a struggling faith. As I teetered there on the precipice, my ability to see or know who I was suffered greatly. And in such moments, I had no clue who was in control.

As a child, we used to tease other kids with the phrase "Your epidermis is showing." In this case, it was my humanity. My human nature (and yours too) is always present, always evident, and therein lies the root cause of dysfunctional behavior and attitudes.

I'll never, ever forget an especially dysfunctional moment in the life of my family. Unfortunately, my oldest son will not either. Somewhere in all the old photos stuffed into boxes are some that tell a sad, sad tale. Kyle and I had driven onto Oceania Naval Air Station in Virginia Beach, Virginia, to take some pictures. Specifically, we were there to get pictures of Kyle, who was all of three or four, perched on the wing of a vintage fighter jet. Cool stuff for this *Top Gun* fanatic.

But Kyle was terrified, and I was a jerk. Instead of letting it go, I forced Kyle to stand on the wing of that plane to get pictures I just had to have. He was the picture of a cute and precious boy— the apple of his daddy's eye. Except that is not the image captured on Kodachrome. No, my son was obviously afraid of heights, and his tyrant of a father couldn't see—wouldn't see—what was being done to him. Anytime those pictures experience the light of day, I am immeasurably saddened by the pitiful little smile he tried to muster through red-rimmed eyes.

Not a banner day for this father without a clue.

The truth is, there are lots more stories I could share. I was far from perfect in any capacity or role I lived. At times, I was hard-nosed, stubborn, arrogant, ignorant, or just plain stupid. ("Stupid" was a bad word in our house, and my mom doesn't much like her oldest talking about himself that way. But there it is.) Any combination of those words—maybe even all of them—could be a pretty apt description of my performance at any given moment.

Some who love me would want to give me more credit than that. But, hey, it's my book, so I can tell it like I see it. I hope that by now you can agree with my assessment: I am a mess!

Oh, how I wish it were all in my past . . . but the reality is that I was a mess, I am a mess, and any foreseeable future I can imagine still has me being a complete and utter mess. Even now as I get the opportunity to refrain from making some of the same mistakes, my messiness rushes back in like an all-American linebacker on a championship team.

Sacked. Again.

There needs to be a twelve-step program for people like me. "Hi. My name is Les Ferguson Jr., and I am a mess. My life is a complete mess, and I am powerless to do anything about it."

Maybe there is a therapy group for people like me. In fact, there is such a group, but we'll talk about that later. If you'll stick with me, I promise we'll get there.

As I began writing what you hold in your hands, I was a real estate salesman. In some ways, it was an easy gig. In others, I wondered if I had lost my mind; or if maybe I could have better supported my family by being the main attraction in the circus freak show. So, rest assured, nothing you will read here has anything to do with being successful, much less a successful businessperson. This is not positive thinking or self-help for the masses.

As I already mentioned, despite my messiness, I used to be a minister and elder in a thriving, exciting, growing church. All my education and training, except for a six-year stint in the U.S. Navy (and maybe even those years too), were preparation for a lifetime of serving God and his people. I had two degrees, a BA in Bible and an MA in New Testament. I had fulfilled the requisites for moving up the ladder to bigger and better things. And yes—wouldn't you know it?—I was also serving myself and my ego.

I'd like to think I am still well-loved. I'd like to know that the good I did far outweighed all the times I messily got in the way of God's work. I wasn't perfect, but I was passionate. Unfortunately, or fortunately, depending on what day of the week it is, that life is now a thing of the past. It was destroyed over a span of about four months. Even during those months, I never saw the end coming until it was over in one, single, solitary moment.

This isn't the story of a preacher whose life imploded over an affair. This isn't about substance abuse or any other scandalous situation you might imagine or concoct. (We love to hear about those who are supposed to be virtuous having the tawdry nature of their lives exposed, don't we?) I wasn't a child abuser or wife beater. For the most part I was just a fun-loving good guy who enjoyed life.

So what then is the story? I thought you'd never ask.

Before Everything Changed

As I've already mentioned, I had joined the navy, got married, had kids, and then decided to be a minister. Life was rocking along. My family grew. We morphed from a military family to being a ministry family. In time, we became a family of six. Mom (Karen), Dad (me), and four boys: Kyle, Cole, Conner, and Casey.

There were definite hiccups along the way. We often struggled financially. Not having our respective extended families close by was difficult at times. But our biggest challenge—our long-term adjustment—was having a mentally and physically handicapped child.

Trevor Cole Ferguson was born November 27, 1989. I loved him as any dad would. When he was diagnosed with cerebral palsy just two weeks shy of his first birthday, I was shattered—for him, for me, for us. In some ways, life would never be the same.

For years I carried hope in my heart. He would grow out of it. Medical treatment would be discovered. And better yet, one day, God would heal him—make him whole, well, and normal, and we would get to see his true potential. I was a dad. I loved him. Can you blame me for wanting those things?

Being the parent of a handicapped child is hard when you see so many other children who will grow up to experience a life yours never can. It becomes a hundred times harder when the chickens come home to roost, and all the little self-delusions that things would change are fully understood for what they are. It's an absence of reality. It's the bitterness of resignation. It happened at Cole's first participation in the Special Olympics. I can still hear those hundreds of handicapped young people and adults thundering out the motto at the start of the games: "Let me win! But if I cannot win, let me be brave in the attempt!"

That was my first full-fledged, "Oh-my-gosh-what-are-we-going-to-do," watershed moment. For the first time ever, I experienced Cole not as a fish out of water, but one in his element. All those kids and adults were just like him. Every worry, fear, and heartache I had imagined was true.

Not to belabor a point, but it was indeed a watershed moment. I felt it physically, emotionally, and spiritually. Life changed. Instead of being a parent of a child who would get better, I was the parent of a son who would be dependent on me forever.

As the days and years went by, more and more we would discover how Cole's disabilities would come to define our lives as a family. Ultimately, we found a way to move forward. Don't get me wrong. There wasn't a grand "aha" moment when every road became straight and we could see where we were going. It couldn't be that easy. Instead, we found a way every day, sometimes multiple times a day.

And, as I said before, life rocked on. We didn't set the world on fire, but we lived, survived, and occasionally thrived. Cole was always a challenge, and we finally made an uneasy peace with that truth. Anything less was to invite even more chaos into our lives.

During this time, my ministry really took off. We struggled through the aftermath of Hurricane Katrina, relief work, and constructing a new church building. It seemed that God was really blessing our work. The church grew by leaps and bounds, and our impact in the community was evident.

Professionally, I wanted more. I earned an MA in New Testament Preaching from Johnson University and had bigger dreams than reality could afford. It took some time and effort on my part, but eventually I made an uneasy truce with my pride and desires and settled in to be a minister. I determined to grow where I had been planted, to use the gifts God had granted. And truthfully? I was great at being a minister, peacemaker, encourager, and leader. I enjoyed preaching from the pulpit. I loved the whole process of studying, thinking, writing, and distilling it all down to one easy applicable point. No long multi-point sermons from this preacher, ever.

And it worked. During those times when the church wasn't growing numerically as I wanted, it seemed that we were growing in knowledge and understanding of self and others. From this vantage point, those were the times when God was preparing us for the next wave or influx of new believers and wounded people.

Make no mistake, ours was a church full of the wounded and disenfranchised. I had naively preached a sermon about my own flaws and hurts, called "I Am a Mess." Here's a short excerpt of what I said:

> I grew up singing about "victory in Jesus," and I must
> tell you that most days I don't feel very victorious! We
> talk about new life, but the truth is, I am a mess. No, I'm
> not addicted to drugs or alcohol, nor have I cheated on
> my wife. But I'm still a mess!
>
> Do you know why I like to wear sweater vests?
> Because I've created this illusion that says when I wear
> one, I don't really look all that fat! And yes, there is
> some pain in that admission. I hate being fat—and even
> though I hate it, most of the time I feel powerless to do
> anything about it.
>
> The truth is, being overweight is not nearly my big-
> gest problem. And since we are being utterly honest
> here, why do so many Christians turn out to be just like
> everyone else?
>
> Why is it that, if you look too close, you'll find a
> living room full of garbage and stink in our lives? Why
> is it that some of us are bitter, angry, and just plain

mean—all the while living under the guise of being
a Christian?

That sermon segued into an unintentional series that eventually
coalesced into a church mission statement of sorts. "No Perfect
People Allowed—Come as You Are" became our identity and
direction. The result was a welcoming church family eager to
embrace any imperfect person who walked into our lives. We were
embodying the message of God: here is forgiveness, acceptance,
and change.

Into this mix of economic and multicultural diversity, anyone
could find a place to call home. We didn't care what you looked
like or where you came from. Dressed up or dressed down, being
a part of our community and family was what mattered. Even
snobs and goody-two-shoes were welcomed, although they often
required more patience, tolerance, and forgiveness than those who
hovered on the fringes of society.

Funny how all of this worked, but ultimately it was not about
the name of the church on the sign out front; it was about belonging to Jesus. To be sure, we preached obedience, but we also
believed in loving people where they were. As far as I was concerned, I was doing my best ministry ever.

This environment fostered the biggest crisis of my life.

———— ⌒ ————

One Single, Solitary Day

"Why, you do not even know what will happen tomorrow. What
is your life? You are a mist that appears for a little while and then
vanishes," James reminds us (4:14).

Everything can change in a moment. That's all it takes for life
to completely unravel. One single day can turn your world, your
life, your existence into something completely unrecognizable.

Chances are that this single day will be completely out of your control. In my case, that day started showing me just how messy life could become.

Maybe you can't point to one moment in your life when the world as you knew it was altered forever. Good for you. Either you have never experienced life ripped asunder, or maybe you did, but through the course of time you absorbed, processed, and moved on to a new existence that has become normal—or, if not normal, at least one you are comfortable with. Either way, I say again, good for you. But if you are still struggling to grasp this concept of a life completely unraveled by events out of your control, I can offer you some instances experienced on a national or regional stage.

- How about Pearl Harbor? I am not old enough to remember the Japanese attack, but in the span of one day, America became a nation destined for a brutal world war.
- I suspect you have your own memories and stories of how life changed and innocence was lost in the morning hours of September 11, 2001.
- I have my own memories of August 29, 2005, when Hurricane Katrina roared ashore and altered for a lifetime the look, feel, and experience of the Mississippi Gulf Coast. Since then, hurricanes by the names of Sandy, Irma, Harvey, and Jose forced their way into our collective consciousness. Each of those names represents one single, solitary day where life not only changed but also became hard and demanding. People went to sleep one night and awoke to a world in which they couldn't buy gas, couldn't flush a toilet, and well, I suspect wherever you live, you get the picture.

When I arrived in my subdivision on the afternoon of October 10, 2011, it was packed with an unbelievable police and paramedic presence. I couldn't get to or see my house, and neither Karen or Cole were answering any of my frantic calls. That and the fact that most of the activity I could see seemed to be centered on my street filled me with dread. I was afraid, and instinctively I knew the worst was at hand. I just didn't yet know how bad it ultimately would become.

Somehow, I knew one life was ending and another was beginning. I stood there in the street making a flurry of phone calls. One to my Dad. One to my friend Doug. And one to my friend Mac. Or, rather, I screamed at them while frantically trying to get a policeman to listen to me.

Finally, the officers did hear me, and in just a few minutes I was surrounded by police protection as they moved me from one place to another for safety until at last I was placed inside an armored SWAT van. Nobody would tell me what was happening. I didn't know where Casey, our youngest son, was. I had been asked to describe my wife, Karen, and son, Cole.

As long as I live, I will never forget seeing the county coroner come around the corner of the van and make his way inside. Unless you've had this experience, you just cannot imagine it. I remember impotently telling him that he wasn't allowed to speak to me—that I knew what he had to say. I wish I had not known, but that freeze frame is frozen forever.

I knew. I knew for sure what my heart had already told me. I knew that what I had already voiced to my father and friends over the phone was my new harsh reality. Ugliness, hatred, and death ruled that day in power, and that power will never be completely broken this side of eternity.

The police investigation pieced together the murderer's pathway through my home as he carried a hatchet and gun. Entering through the garage, he came into our kitchen and living room. Casey, who was five-and-a-half years old at the time, was in my big green recliner reading a book. Cole and my wife Karen also were somewhere in the house.

I will be forever glad that fourteen-year-old Conner was off playing miniature golf with other kids from church that day. I am equally glad that Kyle (twenty-four and married) was building his own life and ministry in Kentucky. Had they been home, the tragedy of that day could have been even worse.

At some point, Casey made it out of the house at his mother's urging as she fought for their lives. We have no real idea how much he saw and experienced. We do know he was in the driveway cradled in the arms of a neighbor when the final two gunshots were fired. Karen and Cole were executed with two shots each in the head. Graphic stuff, I know. More than you may want to know. And I get that. Try having to write those words about your family. It hurt then, and it hurts now. I can't imagine a scenario in this life where those words wouldn't be painfully incapacitating.

But the back story here is even more obscene. I could use more graphic terms in discussing these details, but I will trust that you can read between the lines. I think it's important for you to know something about Cole and Karen's killer and how he got acquainted with our family.

During the spring and early summer, we had invited a kindly looking, seventy-year-old grandfatherly man from our church to care for Cole (now twenty-one years old and still battling cerebral palsy, with an additional diagnosis of mitochondrial disease). We had entrusted him with Cole for a few hours every Wednesday over the course of twelve weeks or so. Cole's mental capacity was that of an elementary-age child, and this arrangement was like having a "friend" over to watch TV with him. During these visits, this man violated Cole in the worst way imaginable right there in our home.

Kids like Cole are high maintenance, which means parents of special-needs kids are often desperate for some downtime. This childcare arrangement was a personal ministry designed so Karen could have some time out of the house. We thought it was a gift from God and eagerly embraced it as such.

During that time, Cole's behavior became very erratic and strange. He was always worried about his DVDs and game discs getting dirty—but he began dumping whole stacks in the sink and running water over them, strangely obsessed with getting them clean. We had no idea what was going on until he finally broke down and told us he had been molested.

Cole also had been threatened that if he told anyone what was happening, his whole family would be shot. During those times of violation, a pistol was laid on his pillow to remind him of the demand to remain silent. We had strong indications that he was forcefully medicated on some of those occasions.

At the time, I thought my son might have been violated once or twice. I never knew until after the double funeral that he had been raped at multiple junctures. It's hard to imagine a scenario that could get any sicker, and as you can imagine, learning about a thing like this is highly traumatic to a parent.

The Aftermath

The months between the perpetrator's arrest and the murders of October 10 were very stressful. We questioned everything, especially our inability to see what was happening to our son. If that wasn't obscene enough, we then began enduring the judgment of a few church members who were indignant because we had reported the crime. I was told I wasn't a real Christian for "not working it out" with the accused. Several of those church members left the congregation. Some began a campaign of rumor, innuendo, and just plain ugliness. One member who I thought was my good friend took the opportunity to attack me for how much I was paid.

The toll on our lives was heavy. There were days I thought I was truly losing my mind. On some days, I was good with that. But somehow, we kept going. Somehow, my ministry stayed afloat. Somehow, we survived and did our best to cope.

But then came the fateful day. I remember much of it as if it was yesterday. Nothing we had already endured in the previous months prepared me for the role of becoming a widower, or worse, for losing a child. I honestly don't know how I got through the first few days. I remember losing time. One minute I was numb; the next minute every nerve ending in my body screamed with agonizing pain. I hurt physically, emotionally, and spiritually. I remember specifically asking one church member if he believed us now. I will never forget having to pick out caskets. The horrors just kept coming. I still feel the ripple effects to this day.

After all of that, a few weeks after the funerals were over, a church lady asked me, "How much pleasure was Cole deriving from his encounters?" I thought for the second time how easy it would be to become a murderer myself. That obscenity made me gag then, and it still does now. Some things should never happen. Or be asked. Or even be imagined.

Three weeks to the day after we laid Karen and Cole to rest, I was approached by a man at church who asked me if I was about to "get over it" and get back to preaching. When I was a child, my friend's father used to tease me by saying one of us was so dumb we were numb. That's probably a bit too charitable for both the question and the questioner.

I know that plenty of the church folks supported me—most likely the clear majority. I know the horror that visited us that day didn't visit just my family—it impacted the entire congregation. And I know people were desperate for things to get back to normal.

After Hurricane Katrina, we kept hearing about having a new normal. Maybe the people around me now could picture their new normal, but not me. Not yet. Not after this. I was a long, long, long way from knowing what my new normal was going to look like. I was constantly experiencing old-normal things in a new, uncomfortable, uncertain, scary, and grief-filled new-normal way.

"Get over it?"

Day after day, long night after even longer night, I was wracked with pain, grief, and an inability to fathom any way forward through the still-descending darkness. Add to the grief and loss the fact that I had been forcefully thrust into the totally unexpected role of being a single parent. Some single parents may make it look easy, but not this guy. It was all I could do to keep the clothes washed, get Conner and Casey to school, and figure out what was for supper. I had never once before even thought of what it would be like all on my own with children to raise. Without any planning or forethought, the ball was squarely in my court. And to add insult to injury, our car insurance company raised my rates because being single at age forty-nine made me a greater danger for risky behavior. Life seemed to get harder with each passing day.

As for preaching? I was so angry and conflicted by all the pain and change that I couldn't think of one decent thing to say about God. My integrity was all I had left, and I could not fake it from the pulpit.

During this time, our family returned to the house where Karen and Cole had been brutally murdered. We had to live there because we had no other realistic options. Before we returned, it had been professionally cleaned by a company that specialized in the removal of blood. But the house had been drenched in a bloodbath, and every time I turned around I was cleaning another patch of bloodstain from walls, door jambs, ceiling, and floors.

Night after night I waited until the kids were in bed asleep, then I scrubbed and scrubbed. I cleaned as quietly and unobtrusively as possible. Spray, rub, scrub, muffled sob. Repeat it. Repeat it again. Each night, I cleaned until the blood splatters were gone from the walls. In the morning, I'd wake up to fresh stains. I cleaned. I painted. And they always came back.

And if these ubiquitous reminders of horror were not enough, imagine the day when I moved the love seat and realized there was a bullet hole in the floor. That was my last day of scrubbing blood-stains. I was done, finished. Ready to go. Ready to leave.

It was time to depart that house—to leave that life, to at least try to make a fresh start. We couldn't escape the memories, but at least we could be someplace where they weren't constantly before us in such vivid Technicolor. Leaving would entail another set of painful changes, but leaving was our best option. So the journey began.

Living with God and the Mess

Truthfully, before this event, I never came close to understanding how dysfunctional and out of whack my entire existence could be. But as I write these words, I have a crystal-clear understanding of how badly life can spiral out of control, both now and in the future. Mine certainly did.

In my pain and anger, I avoided any conversation with God that didn't involve yelling and screaming. I found no comfort in reading Scripture. But then one day, I picked up my Bible and serendipitously found myself reading the story of Jacob wrestling with God. Like a small child constantly asking how or why, I wanted to understand how a man could wrestle with God. Before I knew it, I was wrestling with Scripture. I was delving into the lives of Bible characters, only to see them in a totally different light.

Over the days, weeks, months, and now years that followed, I wrestled with God, wrestled with myself, and wrestled with my faith community. I am still wrestling. I suspect I will be wrestling as I draw my last breath.

In the following pages, you will see me wrestle with God. In some sense, the idea of wrestling with God invokes a word not popular in the dominant culture of today's church. Dare we say the *D* word? *D* is for doubt, and I was wracked with it. It wasn't that I doubted God's existence. No, I doubted whether I mattered to God at all. And if I didn't matter to God, then how could his Word offer any hope to me?

Wrestling with God and wrestling with Scripture required reimagining stories of familiar Bible characters. But more than just revising my view of the stories, wrestling with Scripture meant finding fresh insight into how these characters were like me, or how I was like them. As the similarities became clearer, hope became dearer.

These are their stories. These are my stories. These are your stories, if you choose to see yourself in them.

Chapter 1

PAIN CUBED

*After Nathan had gone home, the LORD struck the child that Uriah's wife
had borne to David, and he became ill. David pleaded with God for the
child. He fasted and spent the nights lying in sackcloth on the ground.
The elders of his household stood beside him to get him up from the
ground, but he refused, and he would not eat any food with them.*

*On the seventh day, the child died. David's attendants were afraid
to tell him that the child was dead, for they thought, "While the child was
still living, he wouldn't listen to us when we spoke to him. How can we
now tell him the child is dead? He may do something desperate."*
—2 Samuel 12:15–18

I hate math. Unless it involves large numbers going into and stay-
ing in my bank account, math isn't something I even want to
consider. And wouldn't you know it? As a former preacher turned
fledgling real estate guy turned preacher again, I need not worry
about dealing with an expanding bank account. Waistline? That's
another story in somebody else's book.

In the meantime, I hate math. Either my mind doesn't get it
or I just don't have the patience to stick with it. If you are a math-
ematician, please don't take this personally, but your passion is not
exciting or stimulating to me. I am not a numbers kind of guy. No,
sir. Bring me a strawberry lemonade cake, and I might change my

mind. But don't try to figure out a formula for that possible equation. For me there aren't any percentages in it.

I called my tenth grader into the room just a few minutes ago so he could explain to me one more time the math concept I want to use here. I think I now understand the concept of a cubed number. Since you may not be the dumbest math person in the world (that's one of my titles, thank you very much), you've most likely got this one down already.

On a scale of one to ten, doctors often want us to tell them how much a wound or infection hurts. I have never had much physical pain. Well, maybe a toothache or two that were excruciating. Several years ago, I cracked a few ribs, broke an elbow, and separated my shoulder all in the same two-handed touch football game.

I was forty-eight years old at the time and determined to keep up with all the twenty- and thirty-something-year-old guys in our Sunday school class. I equipped myself well that day. But on the third interception that I ran back for a touchdown (who's the man?), I got shoved hard, and down I went. I knew I was hurt, and thirty minutes or so after the game was over, I was really hurting.

I slept that night in the recliner, doped up on muscle relaxers. After I preached in discomfort the next morning, one of the docs at church verified the cracked ribs and had me buy a brace for the sprained wrist. Life went on. I continued to hit the gym in the mornings and lift weights. Six weeks later, I was tired of the nagging pain and went to the doctor, where I learned my elbow had been broken the entire time. Three months later? I learned my shoulder had been separated as well.

The moral of the story? Old guys should probably not play contact sports, and my tolerance for pain is much higher than I thought. Or else I am just plain stupid. That may be the case. I mean, how many other knuckleheads lift weights with a broken elbow and a separated shoulder? The truth is, I am not the best guy to use when trying to rate pain on a scale.

But take my story: The multiple rapes of a handicapped boy. The disbelief of those you depend on for emotional, mental, and familial support. The murder of your wife and son and all that came afterward . . . and there is still so much more. The ripple effects never go away. The fallout is still happening. So take all of that and try to put it on a typical pain-tolerance scale. A ten doesn't even come close. There is no chart to plot that kind of pain. Or should I say this kind of pain?

Some days the pain is so great that I have no idea what the end story is going to be. Other days, the pain is more manageable, and I can imagine life in a much better light. But the best way I know to describe the emotional, physical, mental, and spiritual pain my family experienced and still endures is pain cubed.

Here's how it works: If you take a level of pain that is already off the charts and multiply it by itself three times, then you get a pain level whose mathematical quantity is astronomical. Maybe you could find a better way to illustrate it. Maybe you could describe it in a fashion far easier to understand. I'll give you that. But this I promise: unless you have lost a child, you cannot comprehend the level of grief, pain, and suffering I am trying to describe.

Seriously. It is that bad. Factor in all the horror of multiple episodes of rape *and* the shocking brutality of a double murder, and you have moved well beyond anything anybody can easily fathom or describe. This isn't about a contest where we try to decide whose pain is greater. Not my point. Not my intention. And yet, I am grasping at straws to get you to see how badly I hurt, how desperate I was for relief.

Once upon a time, I was a sailor in Uncle Sam's Canoe Club (that's the U.S. Navy, if you can't interpret). Somewhere off the coast of Brazil on our way to Rio, I developed a horrendously severe toothache. We had no dentist or real doctor on the ship. The Chief Corpsman on board had nothing to give me strong enough to mask the pain. At one point, they gave me muscle relaxers to make me loopy—loopy enough to have no idea where I was or why I hurt.

Much of that time I cannot remember. But I do have amazingly total recall of waves of pain so severe (yeah, there's that word again) that they would leave me soaking wet in sweat. If it sounds like bad stuff, it was. But, it was child's play compared to the pain that came with our family tragedy.

I remember telling people I was hurt but wasn't suicidal. ("Liar, liar, pants on fire." Say it at least three times for maximum truthfulness and effect.)

I lied. I am no King David. While his servants were afraid of what he might do in his desperation, the rest of the story tells us of a man who was able to hold it all together. As for me, there were days and moments and times when all I could imagine was how sweet the end of a gun barrel would taste—how cool and comforting would be the final feel of steel between my teeth. The pain was that intense. And debilitating. The pain came in wave after wave that didn't just threaten to overwhelm me. It did. I would literally (and quite figuratively) get up on my feet, and before my equilibrium was restored, down I went again.

Over and over. Again, and again. I grew hoarse from screaming in impotent rage at *the* God (Did you catch "*the* God"? At that point, I wasn't sure if I could call him *my* God) who could have stopped all this but didn't. And they wanted me to preach. To get back to normal. To do whatever I needed to do so they could get back to normal.

The Bible tells us that David washed his face and got back to his life, but it's fair to say that he didn't have great relationships with his kids. It's hard to know exactly how his affair with

Bathsheba and the loss of this child affected David long-term. At least one of my boys has insinuated that I became an absentee father for a time. Is that normal? I don't know how others would react, but when I wasn't screaming, I was emotionally checked out. I knew people were around me. I knew my family was close by. But everything I did, everything I saw, and everything I heard was wrapped up, muffled by a seemingly impenetrable fog. It's hard to emotionally provide for the people you love when you are bereft and empty inside.

I'll never forget that first post-murder Christmas morning opening presents under the tree. We had lots of gifts that year, but only thanks to Amazon. The whole day felt like an out-of-body experience. And that just might be the best way to describe how I interacted with others and, unfortunately, with my children. If you were on the outside looking in, flat and mechanical would have been good descriptions.

Flat and mechanical might have become my new normal had it not been for the spark Becki, my wife now, brought into my life. We had not spoken in more than twenty-five years. She had broken my heart back in those days, and I joined the navy to get away from her. I'll never forget the first time we talked after all those years of no contact. It was like hanging up the phone only to reengage the same conversation the next day. And, just like that, there was something to look forward to. And before I could understand what was happening, I was laughing again. Still sad, still hurting, but learning from her how to see joy again.

There is no going back for me. The hands of time cannot be rewound. All I know how to do is move forward. Sometimes bravely. More times than not, tentatively and fearfully. But the fact that I am moving forward at all should probably be laid at Becki's feet. She fanned the flames of life again, and I will always be grateful to her for the hope and direction she has brought into our lives.

With that out of the way, what follows in this book is not more of what you have already read. What I hope you see is my story in the stories of biblical characters. What I hope you see even more is your story in the lives of biblical characters . . . as they, too, were shaped and changed by their own weakness, but most importantly, by the weakness of God.

GOING DEEPER

Read 2 Samuel 12:15–23

1. How does Les's pain compare to the anguish of David?

2. Is it possible to read either story and misunderstand the nature of God?

3. What else was going on as David grieved?

4. After his son died, do you think David's behavior reflected faith or resignation? How does one survive a story like this without faith?

5. How would you help someone in a situation like Les's or David's?

Chapter 2

THE PAIN OF EDEN

Now the serpent was more crafty than any of the wild animals the LORD God had made. He said to the woman, "Did God really say, 'You must not eat from any tree in the garden'?"

The woman said to the serpent, "We may eat fruit from the trees in the garden, but God did say, 'You must not eat fruit from the tree that is in the middle of the garden, and you must not touch it, or you will die.'"

"You will not certainly die," the serpent said to the woman. "For God knows that when you eat from it your eyes will be opened, and you will be like God, knowing good and evil."

When the woman saw that the fruit of the tree was good for food and pleasing to the eye, and also desirable for gaining wisdom, she took some and ate it. She also gave some to her husband, who was with her, and he ate it. Then the eyes of both of them were opened, and they realized they were naked; so they sewed fig leaves together and made coverings for themselves. —Genesis 3:1–7

There is a side of my personality that likes old things. Old distressed furniture always catches my attention. And cars. I love old cars. Several miles from where I live, a house with a metal carport is surrounded by old cars and scattered junk. In the middle of the mess is an old, faded, red fastback Ford Mustang. I can easily imagine it restored and sitting in my yard. She would be a real beauty.

I like old things. Especially when they have been renewed. One of my favorite passages in all the Bible speaks of the earth groaning in anticipation of being renewed:

> For the creation waits in eager expectation for the children of God to be revealed. For the creation was subjected to frustration, not by its own choice, but by the will of the one who subjected it, in hope that the creation itself will be liberated from its bondage to decay and brought into the freedom and glory of the children of God. We know that the whole creation has been groaning as in the pains of childbirth right up to the present time. (Rom. 8:19–22)

I love this promise of being renewed. Reborn. Remade. Full potential realized. Did you catch that about the pain of childbirth? Many a father-to-be has been shocked by how angry and threatening the sweet mother-to-be can become as she experiences pain that men can only wonder about. Scripture says the pain experienced by creation is the same. Nature groans with the hurt and wait of becoming.

When did this pain begin? All the way back in the Garden of Eden. Adam and Eve were created as perfect beings in a perfect world. Life was good, living was easy, and deceit was unknown. At least until the serpent showed up.

Adam and Eve catch a lot of grief for messing it up for the rest of us. I doubt if any of us could have, would have, done any better. Be that as it may, sin and darkness made an appearance and have been here ever since. Creation groans. We cry. Pain multiplies.

I feel sorry for Adam and Eve. They heard the first lie. And, just like us, they wanted to believe the bill of goods the serpent sold them. They should have believed and trusted in God. They didn't.

We are so often just like them. Repeatedly humanity has acted out the same story in all our lives. Don't blame Adam and Eve. Blame yourself. You make the choices every day to do things God's way or the serpent's way.

God says this. Satan says that. And Satan's "that" always brings pain and unhappiness. If not now, then at least eventually.

For Adam and Eve, the pain was immediate. Suddenly they were kicked out of their paradise home. Suddenly they were sweating, working, striving, and facing the reality of the curse in the very ground around them as they fought to keep their bellies full. And not just their bellies, but the bellies of their children, born in pain and living in struggle. Yes, I feel sorry for Adam and Eve. One ill-advised decision shut down the Horn of Plenty and opened a Pandora's box of suffering. Little did they know it would get much worse.

The first parents ever to grieve the loss of a child? Adam and Eve. The first parents ever to suffer a child being murdered in cold blood? Adam and Eve. The first parents ever to face the punishment of a child who committed murder? Adam and Eve. Can you imagine?

I wonder if they felt the weight of the world on their shoulders. I wonder if they felt like utter failures. I wonder if they second-guessed every single parenting decision they ever made. Can you imagine the conversations?

"What did we do wrong?"

"Where did we fail?"

"What could we have done different?"

"Did he not know we loved him?"

The first couple. The first family. Their son was murdered. Their son was the murderer. Yes, I feel sorry for Adam and Eve.

I am not very good with chronology, and I'm a bit lazy too. I don't know how many years have passed between the story of

Adam and Eve and the story of the man who murdered my family. Let's just keep it simple and say thousands and thousands and thousands of years. Even allowing for all that time and factoring in Noah's story and the destruction of the world by water, I can see a direct descending line from Adam and Eve all the way to my tragedy. As it turns out, our family tree doesn't have nearly as many branches on it as we might imagine.

The man who did the evil things to my family? When it first happened, I hated his guts. He was, to me, the personification of evil. But with time and perspective, I've come to see him as a man just like any of us. When he was born, his parents had hopes and dreams. They had great expectations. Since he was seventy years old when he died, they couldn't have had any knowledge of what he would become. Even so, I can find it in me to feel a bit sorry for the rest of his family.

This part of God's story somehow makes me feel almost sorry for God. Created in his image, living in paradise, Adam and Eve were given one simple job and one small rule to follow, and they blew it. One can almost imagine the heavenly face-palm that must have taken place. One can almost imagine that face-palm is still taking place.

Again, the man who did those evil things to us? He was also a child of God. And because he was, he lived under some simple life directives. As Jesus explained it, the two greatest commandments are to love God and love others. That's all he had to do. That's what we are given to do. Unfortunately, like Adam and Eve and like him, we often give God very little to work with.

Yes, our weakness plays into his weakness. But thankfully, what he doesn't fix now, he fixes later.

GOING DEEPER

Read Genesis 3

1. What were the consequences of the sin of Adam and Eve physically, emotionally, and spiritually?

2. How are those consequences still with us today? Are you ever surprised by the consequences of your sin?

3. Do you think Adam and Eve ever could have envisioned the depths of despair that sprang forth from their sin?

4. How does James 1:13–15 add details to the story of Adam and Eve? Are we still being deceived?

5. What does this phrase mean to you: "Hurt people hurt people"?

Chapter 3

RUNNING

*There was a man who had two sons. The younger one said to his father,
"Father, give me my share of the estate." So he divided his property
between them.*

*Not long after that, the younger son got together all he had, set
off for a distant country and there squandered his wealth in wild living.
After he had spent everything, there was a severe famine in that whole
country, and he began to be in need. So he went and hired himself out
to a citizen of that country, who sent him to his fields to feed pigs. He
longed to fill his stomach with the pods that the pigs were eating, but no
one gave him anything.*

*When he came to his senses, he said, "How many of my father's
hired servants have food to spare, and here I am starving to death! I will
set out and go back to my father and say to him: Father, I have sinned
against heaven and against you. I am no longer worthy to be called your
son; make me like one of your hired servants." So he got up and went to
his father.*

*But while he was still a long way off, his father saw him and was
filled with compassion for him; he ran to his son, threw his arms around
him and kissed him.* —Luke 15:11–20

During at least four periods of my life, running was a major big
deal. In my early forties, I began a successful weight-loss program
that included running three miles every day for about six days a
week. I became addicted. A day without running was never quite

as good as a day when I ran. I learned to love the euphoria often referred to as a "runner's high."

In the aftermath of our family tragedy, I was lost and lonely. I did not know what to do with myself. I wasn't working. I had no direction. I couldn't seem to focus on anything other than pain. And it was all-consuming. Watching TV was out of the question. Every time I turned it on, there was some violent scene that sent me deeper and deeper into my pain. I tried to occupy my time with keeping the house clean, doing laundry, and reading, but I felt as though I was losing my mind.

I desperately wanted to drink myself unconscious. And stay that way. I wanted to stone myself into oblivion. I wanted to know nothing but the peace of blessed nothingness. But I never did any of those things. Not once. Not even a little. But I wanted to. I wanted to do anything that would numb the pain and horror. Anything. I contemplated, as I mentioned before, the taste and feel of cold steel between my teeth. I hurt.

So I ran.

Running for my sanity was a physical thing. I could tie on my shoes, grab my earbuds, and pound the pavement. In the physical exertion of testing and besting myself, I could escape some of the physical, emotional, and spiritual pain that was almost always present.

My running wasn't always pretty. I have always struggled with weight, so you had that to look at. But then, as I ran, I often looked angry and eager for a fight. Because I was. Fortunately or unfortunately, a physical fight with somebody that looked at me funny never quite materialized.

I ran because I was mad. I was mad so I ran. It all depended on the moment.

As for God and me? Those days of running were ongoing fights, rants, and struggles. I ran through a theological minefield. I was desperate for answers. None were forthcoming. Still, I ran.

Therapeutics and questions aside, in my running for relief I finally realized this was a lifelong pattern. Not so much the physical act of exercise, but the whole idea of running from God. I had done this before, maybe for different reasons, but I have lived a lifetime of running from God.

There it is.

I was a preacher's kid. I grew up in church. I was preaching every Sunday by the time I was fifteen. I came of age in the church. I have studied Scripture on both undergraduate and graduate levels, with degrees to show for it. The church was my foundation, security, purpose, and life. But God was an altogether different matter.

If God did all the things I expected, if God fit inside the nice little box that defined the parameters of my life, I was good. But when God required something of me that I wasn't ready to give, I ran.

I have long resonated with the story of Jonah. He was a servant of God who wanted to serve if God's desires reflected Jonah's beliefs and understanding. But as soon as God moved outside Jonah's God-box, he ran. Not toward God, but from God. In a matter of moments, not months, Jonah went from prophet to rebel.

It's easy to judge Jonah. To shake our collective heads with a tsk, tsk, tsk. Jonah blew it, we like to think. But I get it. What God asked of Jonah was painful, illogical, and way outside his comfort zone. What God asked of Jonah challenged his understanding of God. So he ran. It was a self-preservation of sorts.

Like Jonah, running from God, at least in my mind, was a way of protecting me. I had no idea who this God was anymore. In my thinking, God wanted me to accept and serve something fundamentally different from the God I had known before. In the horror of tragedy, he wanted me to trust him. In the horror of tragedy, I was convinced he was unworthy. So, I ran.

My God was going to take care of and protect me. Except he didn't. At least, not in the way I could understand it. So, I ran. While running, I became the prodigal son. Not in the sense of wild living, but in the sense of alienation from my Father. In that respect, I became the elder brother too. I loved God, but I didn't like him one little bit. How could I? From my perspective, he failed my entire family. So, I ran and I argued. I pouted and I blustered. But the problem was, I was running on empty, running blind, arguing with myself, and I had no destination in sight.

I am not exactly sure when it all began to change. I am not sure of the exact timing when I began arguing less with God and looking for something worthwhile. But to put it into a better chronology, it was after I had married again. It was after we had become a blended family. There came a day when it dawned on me that I was failing my children and failing my wife. I was supposed to lead my family into a relationship with God. I was supposed to show them that God came first. I couldn't do that and fight with him too. I had to cry Uncle. I had to go home. I had to realize that God never turned away from me. To the contrary, I had turned away from him.

Remember the story of Onesimus? He was a slave who ran away from his master, Philemon. We are all a little like Onesimus in that we're all running from something. It may be a bad marriage, problems at work, character flaws, or anything we feel powerless to change. But as Onesimus ran, he crashed right into the God who loves runners, the God who not only welcomes them home, but runs with them in the process.

Whether it is Jonah, the prodigal son, or Onesimus, running away solves nothing. Running home? That's another story. Like Onesimus, I had no place to go. I could keep running and get farther away. Or I could own up to the futility of it all, recognize that some things are bigger than me, and make my way, however slowly, home again.

I am particularly fond of this image of God: "While he was still a long way off, his father saw him and was filled with compassion for him; he ran to his son, threw his arms around him and kissed him" (Luke 15:20).

Aren't you glad that God runs too?

GOING DEEPER

Read Luke 15:11–32

1. Do you identify with the prodigal son? How? If so, did your consequences drive you home? Are you in the process of coming home?

2. What catches your attention most about the father? What attributes of God do you see in him?

3. Do you identify with the older brother? How? Are your personal relationships marked by resentment or jealousy?

4. Do you think the older brother had any part in the younger brother's decision to leave home? How is the father a peace-maker in this story?

5. Is coming home worthy of celebration? How or what can you celebrate now?

Chapter 4

THE FAITH OF ABRAHAM?

By faith Abraham, when called to go to a place he would later receive
as his inheritance, obeyed and went, even though he did not know
where he was going. By faith he made his home in the promised land
like a stranger in a foreign country; he lived in tents, as did Isaac and
Jacob, who were heirs with him of the same promise. For he was looking
forward to the city with foundations, whose architect and builder is God.
—Hebrews 11:8-10

Abraham, the father of faith. Or, as the apostle Paul calls him, the
father of all who believe (Romans 4:16 NLT). What exactly does
that mean? What is faith?

In the early days of writing my blog *Desperately Wanting to
Believe Again* (now called *Les Ferguson Jr. Writes*), some might have
been tempted to think I wanted to relearn how to believe in God.
That would be the wrong temptation to embrace. When I used the
word "believe," I didn't mean acknowledging God's existence. To
the contrary, I believed then and believe now—fervently. What I
have wrestled with is faith—the belief and trust that God has my
best interests at heart. That God really does care. That God loves *me*.

Like many of you, I know the scriptural definition of faith:
"Now faith is confidence in what we hope for and assurance about
what we do not see" (Heb. 11:1). I believe that verse. And yet, it is

problematic for me. The first part I am extremely cool with. I have great confidence that God has given me salvation. I eagerly await the day when Jesus comes back to take us home. Notice I didn't say "if"—I said "when." But the second part of the verse gives me great reason to pause and question. Faith gives us "assurance about what we do not see."

I said it was problematic. That's really understating the case. I have found it much too hard to believe that God really wants the best for me. I have struggled significantly with the idea that God was protecting me or taking care of my family. Even now, when I see his providence, I still wonder about the past. I still question the direction of my future.

Whether I wanted it or not, I long ago left my home for a far-away country. I once wrote on my blog that I mourned the loss of me. If we had experienced only a double murder, that would be massively bad enough. But the loss of wife and son, mother and brother, brought on more changes than my struggling little family ever could have imagined.

Yes, I have mourned the loss of me. The connections, the location, the friends, the life I once had. It all went away. And faster than you might believe. I wasn't the first ever to experience such a dramatic change in circumstances. I won't be the last.

I believe Abraham would have understood. God said go and he did. He wasn't given an itinerary. He wasn't told how it would all work out. Worse, we don't get to go behind the scenes to hear the questions and see the worry and fear. We don't even get the satisfaction of knowing there was a hole in his heart when he was leaving one life behind to embark on another. Instead, Abraham, the father of the faithful, is presented as a man who unquestioningly trusted God.

It's a beautiful picture even if it is not quite true. Before you level a charge of heresy or sacrilege, try to remember some stories from his life of faith. It wasn't an all-cheerful Forest Gump "life is like a box of chocolates" existence.

There were struggles. There were hard times. There was disbelief. There was uncertainty. Remember Sarah? Was she wife or sister? And what about the promise of having a son? Sarah laughed. They played pregnancy games. Poor Ishmael was nothing more than a faithless attempt to make God's word come true. And then there was the whole deal of sacrificing Isaac (see Chapter Seven for what I think of this story). Do you really think Abraham made the trip up the mountain with a light heart unburdened by questions, worries, fears, and doubts?

But if none of this is enough to help you see Abraham as a man for whom faith wasn't always easy, then let me remind you of Sodom and Gomorrah. Remember when God was going to destroy those two wicked cities? Remember what Abraham asked the Lord?

> What if there are fifty righteous people in the city? Will you really sweep it away and not spare the place for the sake of the fifty righteous people in it? Far be it from you to do such a thing—to kill the righteous with the wicked, treating the righteous and the wicked alike. Far be it from you! Will not the Judge of all the earth do right? (Gen. 18:24–25)

Abraham wasn't just another yes-man nodding his way through that conversation with God. No, when we read the story, there were questions, doubts, fears, and disbelief. Can you hear them?

I don't know about you, but I can. I hear the questions of Abraham's heart. I see a man of faith who was also a man unafraid to say to the God of the universe, "Hey, wait a minute. I am not sure about all of this. I don't think I understand what you are doing. I see how things aren't working the way I thought they would. Sometimes it doesn't look like you have my best interests at heart. I don't get it at all. And yet, I believe even as I doubt."

In a post-apocalyptic novel, D. J. Molles wrote: "Faith isn't the absence of doubt, it's the decision to believe in something contrary to what you observe."[1] That's a powerful, powerful statement worthy of consideration. In the aftermath of my own tragedy, everything I observed, thought I saw, or even thought I understood led me down a dark path of doubt and distrust. Faith, on the other hand, meant changing my glasses or adjusting my vision parameters so that I could see something bigger or greater or deeper than my current circumstances.

While often overwhelming and life-altering, there is much more to this existence than our momentary difficulties. Learning to change our focus helps us to see the ultimate reality. Struggling or not, we can be like the man who once told Jesus, "I do believe; help me overcome my unbelief!" (Mark 9:24).

GOING DEEPER

Read Hebrews 11

1. How do you define faith? What do you think about the definition the author took from D. J. Molles?

2. Consider the phrase "blind faith." Can faith be blind? If so, when? Does faith have room for doubt or questions?

3. What kind of questions do you think Abraham might have had about leaving his home to go with God? How does faith work in your life?

4. What is the relationship between faith and trust?

5. Sometimes we say things like "if it doesn't work out in this life, it'll work out in the next." How is that belief indicative of a strong faith in God?

Note

[1] D. J. Molles, *The Remaining: Refugees* (New York: Orbit Publishing, 2014), 264.

Chapter 5

THE DON'T-LOOK-BACK MAN

Lot looked around and saw that the whole plain of the Jordan toward Zoar was well watered, like the garden of the LORD, like the land of Egypt. (This was before the LORD destroyed Sodom and Gomorrah.) So Lot chose for himself the whole plain of the Jordan and set out toward the east. The two men parted company: Abram lived in the land of Canaan, while Lot lived among the cities of the plain and pitched his tents near Sodom. Now the people of Sodom were wicked and were sinning greatly against the LORD. —Genesis 13:10–13

Lot, the nephew of Abraham, is a simple character with a complicated life. Part of his complications go far beyond the PG rating of this book, and so there are some things we will not talk about today. At least in mixed company. I turn red far too easily. Plus, I want my mom to read this book. There are some things you just don't want to talk about with Mom.

Most of us know the biblical Lot from the famous account of Sodom and Gomorrah's destruction. In escaping the fire and brimstone that rained down on the twin sin cities, Lot and his family were urged to flee and not look back. If you know how that

55

part of the story ends, you know that Lot's wife failed to heed that final instruction and "became a pillar of salt" (Gen. 19:26).

Long before that incident, Lot was a part of Abraham's journey of faith, and by the time they arrived in the land of Canaan, the Bible says they had too much stuff to stay together in one place. That, and the simple fact that some of their people couldn't keep from fussing and arguing, spurred them to move in different directions.

At the end of Genesis 13, Lot chooses where he is going to live. If you are of a certain church-going age, you most likely heard more than a couple sermons about "not pitching your tents toward Sodom" (KJV). If you don't know the modern word that comes from the name Sodom, don't expect me to explain. Remember what I said earlier? I blush too easily (and Mom is reading). At any rate, Lot sets his family up near a town that is famous for abnormal sexual behavior. Trouble soon follows, although not all of it is of his own making. War breaks out; he and his family are captured and ultimately delivered by Abraham, who rides in to save the day (Gen. 14).

Over the next several chapters in Genesis, Lot is mainly out of the picture. Those chapters are reserved for Abraham's continuing story. If you are following along, we read of the covenant God establishes with Abraham, the birth of Ishmael, the addition of circumcision to the covenant, and the recapped promise of an heir through whom would come a great nation.

And then Genesis 18 happens. The Lord comes to town in the guise of a stranger with two friends, and Abraham goes into hospitality mode. He calls for water, rest, bread, and beef. The language of the Bible indicates this meal wasn't just a slapping together of a quick sandwich. No, these visitors were given fresh baked bread or cakes made expressly for them. No stale leftovers would suffice! Can you smell the steaks sizzling on the fire? This was a feast worthy of honor. This was an example of true hospitality to strangers and wayfarers.

Soon enough, the meal was complete. The promise of a son was unexpectedly reiterated. And then, God tells Abraham of his plans to judge Sodom and Gomorrah. So, the same Uncle Abraham who had rescued Lot before suddenly learned that he was again in mortal danger. God had apparently had enough of the wickedness of Sodom and Gomorrah. His reason for visiting Abraham was to alert him to the possibility of total annihilation. Abraham was horrified by the prospect. Bargaining with God over the destruction of these cities, Abraham sought to save those who might be considered righteous—and we might suspect that Lot and company were foremost on his mind.

I bet you didn't start this chapter thinking you'd get a play-by-play of Lot's Sodom and Gomorrah escapades, but here we are. In Genesis 19, it is Lot's turn to entertain the aforementioned strangers, and the differences in the story are telling. Lot, of course, offers hospitality, but it all seems quite stressed and anxious. In hindsight, one gets the distinct impression that Lot knows what is coming and is trying desperately to salvage the whole situation.

Lot invites them in with the stated purpose of sending them away early the next morning—again, attempting to avoid any trouble. But these strangers intend to sleep in the town square. The Bible says of Lot: "But he insisted so strongly that they did go with him and entered his house. He prepared a meal for them, baking bread without yeast, and they ate" (Gen. 19:3).

Do you see the worry? Can you hear the near panic in Lot's voice? And did you catch the major difference between the feast Abraham prepared and what Lot had to offer? Abraham's meal was sumptuous. Lot's meal was hurried, as if to limit the time spent with these two strangers.

Even though Lot was a relative newcomer to this community, I suspect he'd been there long enough to know what was coming next. And it did. Men from the town showed up seeking carnal knowledge of Lot's visitors. Unfortunately, their behavior sealed the deal. The two visitors saw firsthand what they needed to know.

Poor Lot. I wonder if he spent a lot of time before this incident second-guessing his fateful decision. I wonder if he regretted "pitching his tent toward Sodom" because "he had seen that the land was well-watered and like a garden of the LORD" (Gen. 13:10). I wonder if he recognized how his pride, greed, and materialism had brought him to live in this evil place.

How's that?

We typically see the sin of Sodom and Gomorrah as aberrant sexual behavior. We focus on that and see nothing else. From that perspective, the story of Lot has for many, many years served as warning to individuals and societies alike not to cross certain thresholds. It doesn't take much news watching or television viewing to know that this cat has been out of the bag for a long while. And while we sometimes fret and wail over a lifestyle far outside our comfort zones, we have so fixated on the wrong thing that we may have completely missed the real point of the story—or the real problem in Sodom and Gomorrah.

I am a lot like Lot in that respect. I may not be guilty of certain behaviors that I don't even really understand. I may live in a perilous peace with some wicked forces and woes. And I may be very much a part of the problem.

While writing this chapter, I took a break from writing and visited the cell phone store. While I was there, I remarked to the customer service rep who was helping me that there sure were a bunch of shiny bright tech toys to choose from. Frankly, I had no need or desire for anything lining the shelves or on the walls. But after just a few minutes of casually glancing around the store,

I suddenly found myself wanting any number of those electronic enticements.

Why? I didn't need any of them. I wasn't missing out on anything. But I was wowed by the dazzling new designs, and soon I was thinking it sure would be nice to have another speaker . . . or a different case . . . or a better set of headphones . . . and while we are at it, the latest iPhone would be nice too. Let's also not forget that there is also a newer version of the Apple watch available as well!

See how quickly we get caught up in the power of stuff? Do you think it possible that Lot chose his living arrangements based not solely on distance from his Uncle Abraham, but in some part on the proximity to those things that satisfied his own pride, greed, and materialism?

There is always the very real sense that all our sin is based on selfish desire, but what if we could point to a specific attitude, behavior, or frame of reference? What if the aberrant behavior Sodom is infamous for was just a symptom of a bigger problem? Even worse, what if that bigger problem is just as prevalent today? And if it could get worse than "even worse," what if that bigger problem is not only rampant in our culture, but symptomatic in me or in you?

Here's where our defense mechanisms try to take charge. Here's where we announce loudly and emphatically that we are not aberrant sexual predators and therefore innocent of any suggested similarity. And in the very best fake French accent I can type with, "aw kontraire," my friend. There is more to the sins of Sodom than meets the already-jaundiced eye.

In the book of Ezekiel, the prophet explains the sins of Judah. In doing so, he gives voice to the failures and sins of some of her neighbors: "Now this was the sin of your sister Sodom: She and her daughters were arrogant, overfed and unconcerned; they did not help the poor and needy. They were haughty and did detestable things before me. Therefore I did away with them as you have seen" (16:49–50).

Sweating yet?

I have plenty of food to eat. In fact, you could easily make a case against me for gluttony. I crave security. My pride is almost always evident. I have been trained and conditioned by culture and society simply not to see those who are hurting and less fortunate than I am.

But haughty and detestable? Come on, God, really? Yes, haughty and detestable is that attitude and behavior that sets me up as a higher authority. Haughty and detestable is the belief that I can do whatever I want. Haughty and detestable is the conviction that even the laws of nature do not matter to me, were I to choose to flaunt them.

As it turns out, I am a lot like Lot and maybe even more like Sodom. And yes, I am sweating. I am sweating because before my family tragedy I thought more highly of myself than I should. I was arrogant and prideful. I was my own authority—but worse than that, after my tragedy, I was more so. If God wouldn't do what I thought he should, then God must not really matter all that much.

Whether it is from tragedy or our own sin, pain can warp our thinking and twist our understanding of God. Warped and twisted makes for a very dark path. I shudder to think what my life would be like had I not seen how deeply flawed and broken I had become. As it turns out, my tragedy simply shined a light on the brokenness that was already there.

If I am Lot, I suspect you are too. Don't wait for a tragedy to reveal your flaws and deficiencies.

GOING DEEPER

Read Genesis 19

1. If you heard someone say, "He's a prince of a guy," would you think of Lot? Why or why not?

2. Why did Lot choose to live near Sodom and Gomorrah? What do his choices say about ours?

3. Do you think it possible Lot became numb to his environment? Do we become so accustomed to the wickedness around us that we make a tenuous peace where we shouldn't?

4. Is materialism a problem in your life? Does what you own breed a haughty spirit? Does your failure to speak or take action on behalf of others put you in the detestable column?

5. Are you your own standard for what is good and right? What is it you crave enough that you would take shortcuts or liberties with your own character to acquire it?

Chapter 6

FEELING FORLORN AND FORGOTTEN

She put the boy under one of the bushes. Then she went off and sat down about a bowshot away, for she thought, "I cannot watch the boy die." And as she sat there, she began to sob.

God heard the boy crying, and the angel of God called to Hagar from heaven and said to her, "What is the matter, Hagar? Do not be afraid; God has heard the boy crying as he lies there. Lift the boy up and take him by the hand, for I will make him into a great nation."
—Genesis 21:15–17

I know tears. Some days it seems as if my whole world is made of tears. Don't ask me to cry you a river. I've been there and done that more times than I care to remember. Better yet, each of my tear rivers has its own name.

The river *I'm-screaming-at-you-God-and-why-won't-you-answer?* Or the river *This stinks.*

The river *Will it ever quit hurting?* Or the river *Why didn't you stop this?*

Tributaries, streams, creeks, and cricks feed all those rivers and more with names like *Hurt, Pain, Anger,* and *Frustration.*

Do you know where it all ends up? In the vast, big, huge ocean called *Grief.*

Grieving as a process has been around ever since Adam and Eve snagged a bite of the forbidden fruit. They began a new river of tears that day, and that river became a raging torrent when one son murdered another. For whatever reason, I grieve. You grieve. We all grieve. Not yet, you say? Keep breathing and eventually grief will find its way to you.

I wrote these words on my blog, *Desperately Wanting to Believe Again*, when we passed the two-year anniversary of Karen and Cole's murder:

October 10, 2013.

Not today. But Thursday. This Thursday. Not tomorrow. Not Wednesday. Thursday.

It's coming quickly. More quickly than we want. We would like to fast forward past it. Better yet, skipping it completely seems like a splendid idea. But no matter how badly we want to avoid it, it's coming like gangbusters and will continue to do so until time is no more.

With every day of every calendar. With every new moon of every month. With every change of every season, it comes around again and again.

For most folks, October 10th is just another fall day. The sun will rise. The day will run its course. And a new day will take its place.

This year it is on a Thursday. A prelude to a three-day weekend. The boys have various things planned or hoped for. We need to get in another load of firewood.

Life goes on.

This October 10th means two years.

Two. Two years. Two long years. Two short years. Two heartbreaking years.

Two years of pain.

Two. Two years. Two years of happiness. Two years of joy. Two years we could not have ever imagined.

Two years of new life and living. Two years of new experiences. Two years of new relationships. Two years of new challenges. Two years of new adventures.

Two. Two years of struggle. Two years of triumph.

Two. Two years of wondrous healing. Two years of still desperately needing to be healed.

Two. Two years seems like an achingly long time with more to come. Two years is an eternity.

Two years have passed in an incredible blur. Two years gone, and it seems like the past was a dream life barely remembered.

Two. Such a paradox. Such is life.

Two years ago, this coming Thursday, October 10, 2013, one life ended and another began.

What do you do with an anniversary like this? What do you do with a yearly reminder of the most hurtful, pain-filled day in your life and the lives of your children?

Two years and an ocean-full of tears. Two years and a heavy heart.

Two years . . .

This Thursday we remember. Not that we ever forget. But this Thursday we remember.

We remember, honor, and give thanks. We give thanks for the lives we lived and those we lost. We give thanks for the new lives we live and the new love we've found.

And we endeavor. We endeavor to live life fully. We endeavor to embrace every day. We endeavor to face the future while never forgetting the past.

Two. We remember.

Here we were two years later (and now even more than that, as slowly as I write). In some respects, we have made tremendous strides, but in others? I'm sometimes weary of ever having any kind of career again. I wonder if I will ever experience job security or know the thrill of a regular paycheck.

Yes, I have already established the river or stream called *Frustration*. Its banks are full. I remain frustrated. These days it seems as if I am working on another river called *Forlorn* or *Forgotten*.

The longer I stay frustrated, the more it feels as if I am all alone, forlorn and forgotten. Forgotten by the God I desperately want to believe has my best interests at heart. I am hardly the first ever to have felt that way.

Do not withhold your mercy from me, LORD;
    may your love and faithfulness always protect me.
For troubles without number surround me;
    my sins have overtaken me, and I cannot see.
They are more than the hairs of my head,
    and my heart fails within me.
Be pleased to save me, LORD;
    come quickly, LORD, to help me.

May all who want to take my life
    be put to shame and confusion;

may all who desire my ruin
>   be turned back in disgrace.
May those who say to me, "Aha! Aha!"
>   be appalled at their own shame.
But may all who seek you
>   rejoice and be glad in you;
may those who long for your saving help always say,
>   "The LORD is great!"

But as for me, I am poor and needy;
>   may the Lord think of me.
You are my help and my deliverer;
>   you are my God, do not delay. (Ps. 40:11–17)

As long as time continues, I draw no comfort from the certain knowledge that I will not be the last to cry this prayer. Forlorn. Lonely. Forgotten. Passed over. Overlooked. Ignored. Unimportant. All those words describe how I have felt; all those words describe how I am feeling. If you give me a few minutes, I'll probably think of some more.

In the meantime, I am reminded of the story of Hagar and Ishmael. This story begins with a promise from God to Abraham and Sarah. A son will be born to you. A son of promise. The future of a great and amazing nation of people will come through you. If Abraham was like me, I suspect he could hardly wait to see how it all played out.

Except it didn't. At least not according to his time frame. Abraham was seventy-five when God called him to leave his country, when God made him a promise of a son. He was ninety years old when God renewed his promise. He was a hundred years old when God finally fulfilled the promise.

That's a lot of waiting.

What does time do when you are forced to wait? Ask any kid who is watching the clock and waiting for the last bell to ring. Ask the child who is counting down the days until Santa Claus arrives. It drags. Sometimes on and on. Sometimes it drags on long enough for major misgivings and doubt to arise. Sometimes it drags on to the point where you feel as if you must take matters into your own hands.

Take Sarah, for example. Childless, desperate Sarah must have been beside herself when she conspired to have her husband have a child with her slave woman, Hagar.

Poor Hagar. Already a slave, she became the first surrogate mother, only to find herself locked into a bitter struggle with Sarah, her mistress. In time, she gave birth to Abraham's son, Ishmael. But he was not the promised one.

Eventually Isaac was born. Here was the Son of Promise. The Hope for the future. The beginning of what would become the great nation of Israel. But what of Ishmael? As I said in an earlier chapter, poor Ishmael was nothing more than a faithless attempt to make God's word come true.

Yes, Sarah played that game too, but eventually Sarah had had enough of the drama. Isaac was here. There was no room for the pretender. So Abraham did what any loving, kind husband and father does. He abandoned one wife and son for another. The Bible tells us Abraham was distressed by all this. And while he did have assurance from God that all would be right in the end, poor Hagar was physically and emotionally set adrift.

Discarded. Cast off. Deserted. Dumped. Can you imagine how Hagar and Ishmael might have felt? Wandering and alone in the desert? Can you imagine the fear of abandonment? Can you imagine the terrifying pain of what-do-I-do-next? Can you imagine the gut-wrenching moment when it seemed all was lost? Can you imagine Hagar in the moment she recognized her inability to save her son?

You can, can't you? You recognize the feeling of hopelessness? You recognize the feeling of being lost and alone? Yeah. I get that in spades. Life happens to us all. And when it happens to you, remember this: you are not alone. And just as God heard Hagar, he hears your cries too. I love these words from Lamentations:

> I have been deprived of peace;
>> I have forgotten what prosperity is.
> So I say, "My splendor is gone
>> and all that I had hoped from the LORD."
>
> I remember my affliction and my wandering,
>> the bitterness and the gall.
> I well remember them,
>> and my soul is downcast within me.
> Yet this I call to mind
>> and therefore I have hope:
>
> Because of the LORD's great love we are not consumed,
>> for his compassions never fail.
> They are new every morning;
>> great is your faithfulness.
> I say to myself, "The LORD is my portion;
>> therefore I will wait for him."
>
> The LORD is good to those whose hope is in him,
>> to the one who seeks him;
> it is good to wait quietly
>> for the salvation of the LORD. (3:17–26)

As it turns out, I am a waiter, waiting on the Lord.
We can wait together, can't we?

GOING DEEPER

Read Genesis 21:1–21

1. Think about Christmas as a child. Do you remember the gift you had to have? If you didn't get it, how did you react?

2. Think of one big thing you begged God for? Did you receive it? How do you handle disappointment?

3. How do you feel when you see the prayers of others answered positively and yours are not? Do you feel rejected, bitter, angry, or lost?

4. Have you ever felt abandoned and crushed? What would you have said to Hagar in her abandonment?

5. What does it mean to wait on the Lord?

Chapter 7

NOT BORN RETARDED

Some time later God tested Abraham. He said to him, "Abraham!"
   "Here I am," he replied.
   Then God said, "Take your son, your only son, whom you love—
Isaac—and go to the region of Moriah. Sacrifice him there as a burnt
offering on a mountain I will show you." —Genesis 22:1–2

I was taught through much of my life that it was wrong to hate anything. But I do. You may be tempted to think I hate the man who murdered my family. I tried to. I want to even now. Sometimes, I think I feel the need to hate him. But the truth is it takes too much energy and time to keep hatred stoked and burning. I knew the man but for a short time. With apologies to those who may have loved him, it's best for my well-being just to let him go. He is in the hands of God, and however God works that out is his business.

   On the other hand, being fully human, I claim inconsistency. Like you, I have many inconsistencies in my life. Some things I hate with a passion. I hate the word "retarded." And that's probably the largest understatement you'll read today.

   If you ever feel the need to have your insides pulled out through your nostrils (trying to be as descriptive as I can without being profane or obscene), let the parent of a mentally challenged

71

or handicapped child hear you calling their kid "retarded." Or describing them as someone who rides "the short bus."

I hate the word "retarded." I hate it because that was how so many saw Cole and others like him. I am not in denial. I know he was mentally and physically limited. (But, hallelujah, no more!) But despite those limitations, he was worthy of respect and love. He was a good boy who didn't deserve the horrors that befell him— even the one that afflicted him from birth.

The bitter truth is that we are all limited in some fashion or another. Not even one of us is a perfect physical specimen without flaws. And that's just on the outside. In our hearts and minds, in our thinking and attitudes, we all are less than what God intended.

I know Cole had a limited mental capacity. But that word I hate? No parent should ever have to hear their child referred to or thought of in that way. It makes me nauseated to think, say, or even consider it. I know how the world saw him. But those who knew him best saw the incredible gift of ministry and love he gave to the world. They saw him shine!

Many years ago, when I was a youth minister, Cole was my greatest asset. He brought those kids together like nothing else could. I am proud he is my son. Being handicapped was just another example of the weakness of God. God could have healed him, but he didn't. And still God was at work in Cole's life and, through Cole, in the lives of others.

Reading through the pages and stories of the Bible, we find no characters that are mentally incapacitated at first sight. But the truth is, any number of characters were damaged goods—and by damaged, I mean in the way we would look at them. Take David as one example. God called him a man after his own heart. We know him as a dysfunctional husband, father, and leader. And still, he did great things for God and his chosen people.

So there is a sense in which you could call every person in the Bible—other than Jesus, of course—somewhat dysfunctional at best, stunted in the middle, and retarded at worst. I'd like you to consider the story of Isaac in that light. Can you imagine what it must have been like living with Abraham, the father of the faithful? Can you hear Abraham having this conversation with his son?

> "You know, son, back in my day, when God spoke, we listened. He said 'go' and we went. He said 'leave' and we left. He said, 'You're gonna have a son who will be the child of promise and a whole nation will come from him.' That's you, boy. And in just a few minutes we are gonna load up and head up that mountain to offer a sacrifice. And don't you worry your little head one bit. You carry the firewood and God (said in a voice like Jerry Clower, Gaaawwwd) will provide the sacrifice."

Do you remember the old sitcom *Different Strokes*? Gary Coleman had a signature line he would use on his brother: "What you talking about, Willis?" In my crazy imagination, I hear Isaac saying something similar, especially around the time he realizes that he's the sacrifice his father is offering.

How old was Isaac when this episode occurred? There is vast disagreement. Some say between eighteen and twenty years old. Others around thirty-three years old. The Jewish historian Josephus says he was twenty-five years old. And still others believe he was around thirty-seven. The one thing they all agree on? Isaac was no small boy when this incident happened—a small boy couldn't have carried the wood needed for such a large sacrifice.

However you read it, can you try to imagine all of this from Isaac's perspective? Can you imagine that an incident like this might have stunted your relationship with your father? With both of them? Can you imagine that when it came to all things

God-related, Isaac might very well have become *imbecilic?* Seriously, think about it. How do you maintain a good relationship going forward when you were the object lesson used in testing your father's faith? How do you relate to God when he used you in such a way?

All of that, and I am still wrestling along with Abraham. I'd love to know what was going through his head all those years of living with and for the Lord. Back in Chapter Four, I made this statement: "Abraham wasn't just another 'yes man' nodding his way through that conversation with God. No, when we read the story, there were questions, doubts, fears and disbelief. Can you hear them?" Honestly? I am still trying to listen. Maybe I have it all wrong, but I cannot imagine that all the changes, difficulties, and directions God took Abraham through weren't met with some amount of background doubt.

Just take the promise of a son, for example. We know from Scripture that Sarah schemed to make the promise come true (Gen. 16). We know that Abraham laughed at the idea (Gen. 17). And we know Sarah was laughing about it too (Gen. 18). And yet, at the age of one hundred (Abraham) and the age of ninety (Sarah), they became the proud parents of a bouncing baby boy we know as Isaac.

After all that drama, confusion, and the years of wondering and waiting, God says go kill your boy? We are told in Hebrews 11:19 that Abraham had "reasoned that God could even raise the dead." If you are reading this book, chances are the idea of a bodily resurrection is something you've always known about. But how could Abraham have known?

From our vantage point, we know God never intended for Isaac to be killed by his father. But Abraham's questions notwithstanding, it was a tied-up Isaac at the pointy end of the knife. Once Abraham raised the knife in the air, Isaac's entire life was under question. Who am I? Who is my dad? What kind of a God do we serve?

Would you blame Isaac if he spent the rest of his life licking his wounds from such an ordeal? Or, would you expect him to move forward as if nothing ever happened? While he wasn't born that way, I suspect Isaac was fundamentally and functionally retarded from that point on. At best, he was damaged goods with a whole host of issues to deal with.

Despite it all, Isaac was still a part of God's plan.

So am I.

So are you.

GOING DEEPER

Read Genesis 22:1–14

1. When you read the story of Isaac's sacrifice, how do you see him? As a small child, a teenager, or an adult?

2. Do you think Isaac had more questions for his father as they journeyed up the mountain than those you read in the text? What would your questions be?

3. How would you describe the trust between Abraham and God? Between Isaac and Abraham?

4. Do you think living with a father like Abraham who was so willing to act on his faith made him a hard act to follow?

5. With all due respect to those with family members who are mentally challenged, do you think Isaac would have had mental or emotional problems after this event? Is it possible he may have struggled the rest of his life? Why do you think that? Or why not?

Chapter 8

THE TRICKSTER

That night Jacob got up and took his two wives, his two female servants and his eleven sons and crossed the ford of the Jabbok. After he had sent them across the stream, he sent over all his possessions.

So Jacob was left alone, and a man wrestled with him till daybreak.
—Genesis 32:22–24

By now you are aware of my family's story. Like the ripples from pebbles thrown in a pond, they go on and on, and we will deal with the implications for the rest of our lives. Recovery is hard, hard work. It means learning to cope, survive, rebuild, and thrive while moving beyond grief and destruction into new life. From my perspective, the ability to impart some of my journey may be the best way to honor the past, look to the future, and reconcile with God.

Be sure to know I am angry with God. Still. Even as I write these words. He has heard, felt, and seen my wrath. I have questions. He has answers. Thus far, he has been less than forthcoming in sharing them. And yet, he has been gracious and patient as I wrestle and struggle with him.

In the meantime, did you know that a whole mega-billion-dollar industry is fueled by untold masses who are either in touch with their inner boy—or better yet, their inner redneck? It's called professional wrestling, and it features some amazing characters with even crazier names. How about the bogeyman or the Bastion Booger? (Bet his mother's proud!)

One of my favorite characters, and maybe the one I most identify with, could have held his own on the professional wrestling circuit. And his name is worthy of the WWE. He was the patriarch Jacob, whose name means "trickster"! He really lived up to his name. The day he was born, he came into the world using the famous heel hold on his seconds-older twin brother, Esau. And that was just the beginning of a lifetime of trickery, treachery, manipulation, and wrestling.

Over the course of Jacob's life, he schemed and defrauded his way into positions of power and blessing—most notably, making his brother Esau the victim. Eventually, his behavior caught up with him, and he fled for his life. For a while, he met his match in his father-in-law, Laban. The story of how Laban tricked Jacob into wedding two wives (substituting one sister for another) tells us Jacob wasn't nearly as smart as he thought.

But turnabout is fair play, and eventually Jacob with a little more trickery increased his own wealth at the expense of his father-in-law. Then it was time for Jacob to come home and face his brother Esau. Years had passed, and Esau had become a force to be reckoned with. Jacob was justifiably afraid. His fear led him to try familiar behavioral patterns. It was time to manipulate his homecoming. So he sent emissaries ahead. He bribed with livestock. Esau was not dissuaded. He came to meet Jacob in the company of four hundred warriors. As a last resort, Jacob sent his wives and children across the river to safety and prepared to meet Esau alone the next morning.

I read this story and I am left to scratch my head and question. What was going on? Did Jacob truly wrestle with God all night long? And prevail? Because it looks for all the world like

Jacob held his own with God. At least until God had enough and decided to get Jacob's attention. How could that be? How could an old man wrestle with the divine and somehow hold on, if not prevail, all night long? Can you at least agree that there is something here worth understanding?

This story of Jacob wrestling is a sign or symbol of his entire life. Jacob had been a man of destiny before his birth, but somehow he was never content with trusting God. In that regard, Jacob is every man and every woman. We all find ourselves attempting to make deals with God, bargaining for righteousness, bartering for grace, earning what can't be earned.

His entire life was built on trickery, treachery, manipulation, and wrestling.

And weakness. We can't forget weakness. But it's not Jacob's weakness we are considering; it's God's weakness. You see, the only logical, rational answer to Jacob's prevailing with God is weakness.

Not that God is weak, but that God chooses weakness or restraint. (For another example, think of Jesus on the cross.) Throughout Jacob's entire life, God could have stopped, changed, or altered the process and outcome of Jacob's actions. But God didn't. Not until the end of a long night of wrestling did God show his strength. And it changed everything.

When you come into the presence of God in a life-altering way, you might limp away a cripple, dependent on God for what we cannot do ourselves. I wish I had learned some of these lessons in an easier fashion. But I didn't, and that's that. So here I am. Like many of you, the product of trauma. Of grief. Of heartache. A limping shell of the man I once was.

Except that's not quite true. You see, after Jacob's long night of wrestling, after the pain of the crippling blow, he still hung on. By a thread? Yes! By the tiniest of margins, Jacob hung on. That's what each of us must do when faced with the hardest—hang on.

Wrestling with God has become a life-describing metaphor for me. In the process, hanging on is often so incredibly hard to do. I wish I could be like Jacob and point to one single solitary night of grappling and struggling with God. That would be so very convenient, at least for me. Unfortunately, my wrestling match is still ongoing. Frankly, I want to scream and holler, "Fix it, Jesus"—and one day he will. In the meantime, I wrestle and I limp.

I am not predisposed to an automatic, no-holds-barred (see that wrestling term I snuck in there?) trust of God. That's a part of my wrestling. What I am preconditioned to is automatic questioning and doubt. That's my limp. At every setback, I question and ponder. With every new implication or struggle, I wonder why. To borrow a common phrase, I know God never promised me a rose garden, but the constant thorns surely do make me limp. On my best days, I shine, but on my worst, it's all I can do to hang on.

But hang on is what Jacob did, and God blessed him with a new name, a new identity, a new way of life. No longer the trickster, Jacob's new name *Israel* means "God struggles." And whether it was the man Israel, the nation Israel, or the new spiritual Israel, God wrestles to help each of us become what he intends.

So join me in striving to hang on, because God invites the struggling and those who wrestle. It is his nature. Don't get me wrong. He may or may not restore all your fortunes. Life may never be as good as you once thought. Some things are not fixable on this side of eternity. Nevertheless, we may yet—through the fire and pain, through the wrestling and doubt—limp through to the other side and, in the words of the beloved hymn, declare. . .

And Lord, haste the day when my faith shall be sight,
The clouds be rolled back as a scroll;
The trump shall resound, and the Lord shall descend,
Even so, it is well with my soul.

GOING DEEPER

Read Genesis 32:22–32

1. How would you describe Jacob's character? Would you deem him trustworthy?

2. Have you ever been swindled or conned or manipulated? How did that feel when the deceit came to light?

3. How well do you trust others?

4. What does it say about God that he would use the dubious character of Jacob to fulfill his plans?

5. What are you wrestling with God about? Are you approaching him in complete honesty? Is there a hidden agenda in your life that needs to be faced head-on?

Chapter 9

MR. DREAMY

Joseph had a dream, and when he told it to his brothers, they hated him all the more. He said to them, "Listen to this dream I had: We were binding sheaves of grain out in the field when suddenly my sheaf rose and stood upright, while your sheaves gathered around mine and bowed down to it."

His brothers said to him, "Do you intend to reign over us? Will you actually rule us?" And they hated him all the more because of his dream and what he had said. —Genesis 37:5–8

Writing is sometimes a pleasure, sometimes a chore. And sometimes, writing brings a certain catharsis, yes, a sweet release. But as we journey along together looking at biblical characters from a different perspective, I keep seeing myself. And as I see myself in these stories and images, I am not recoiling in horror. Nor do I feel any superiority or find any reason for smugness or arrogance. But I see myself in each character. I feel his pain. I share the struggle. I am just as human as every person we've studied. Maybe because of that, the story of Joseph resonates with me. His story assures me that I am not alone. And neither are you.

In my Bible, an editor-supplied heading atop the scripture you read above says: "Joseph Dreams." Without reading or knowing the story, without knowing the events that follow, without even a smidgen of understanding as to the role Joseph played in the great story of God, I get him. I get Joseph because I get dreaming. I am a dreamer.

For years, I dreamed of living a long successful life with a house full of joy, laughter, and beauty. I dreamed of financial independence. I dreamed my children would all be well and well-supplied. I dreamed that my son Cole would be healed, normal, and living life to the fullest. I dreamed about writing and publishing. I dreamed about being this exceptional preacher. I dreamed about having the admiration and respect of my peers, and maybe, just maybe, even being the subject of some envy. These dreams remained persistent over the years. As Nancy Wilson of Heart would sing, "These dreams go on when I close my eyes."

Maybe you are a dreamer too. Poor Joseph was a dreamer, but his dreams just didn't fit the reality his brothers envisioned.

Talk about a dream-killer. Joseph's brothers had had enough. By selling Joseph into slavery, they propelled him into a life of adventure far greater than most of us can imagine, or even dream about. Joseph did indeed live to see his original dream about his brothers come to pass. He experienced that and so much more. But the journey there was far from easy. It involved false accusations. It led to time in prison—and not the country club camp variety. It meant audiences before the king. It was written in high drama and stress. And it culminated in his becoming the second-highest power and authority in all the land of Egypt.

I just love a story with a happy ending, and this one certainly qualifies. But more than just a story of happy endings, it is also a story of pain. It is a story of betrayal, and betrayal again. It is a story of lies. Indeed, it is a story of heartache and fear. It is a story of questions, doubt, and uncertainty. Those were all ordeals Joseph had to walk through, walk with, and walk in spite of to get to the happy ending. But there is something here worth remembering. Or acknowledging. Or even learning again.

Maybe your dreams have been smashed. Maybe a dream-killer has writ large across the pages and dreams of your life. Maybe there is nothing in your life that remotely resembles what you once dreamed. Remember when I said *I am not alone*? Neither are you. But if I could offer you some hope out of my own deep reservoir of pain and suffering, this is what I would say . . .

Don't be afraid to dream again. Don't. Be. Afraid.

Maybe your dreams will change. Maybe they will reflect a new reality. Maybe they will be less *wow*-worthy than before. Maybe they will end up being more extravagant than you could have dreamed before. Don't be afraid to dream again.

And my dreams? They are mostly still the same. They have worked out differently, but they have taken me to a place of familiarity.

I dreamed of living a long, successful life with a house full of joy, laughter, and beauty. Some of the old dream still exists in my surviving children. But God has seen fit to bring a new family into existence. Part old, part new, and full of joy, laughter, and beauty. I dreamed of financial independence. I am still waiting on that, but frankly, I am content. I dreamed my children would all be well and well-supplied. And thus far they are. They may not have everything they want, but life is good.

I dreamed that Cole would be healed, normal, and living life to the fullest measure. I dreamed, prayed, dreamed, and prayed some more. And that dream or prayer was answered. Not how I intended, but in a way that is ultimately far more than what my limited vision could see.

I dreamed about writing and publishing. I dreamed about being this exceptional preacher. I dreamed about having the admiration and respect of my peers . . . and maybe even being the subject of some envy. I don't know about publishing, envy, or admiration, but here I am. I am writing, and it is far surpassing my wildest dreams.

A part of me wants to walk around asking people to pinch me. Am I awake? Is this really happening? I am quite surprised because my dreaming is becoming more daring by the day. God is pushing me through the what-ifs of my dreams *and* the reality of my present situation to be a bit bolder, to not be so tentative. It's not that I don't still wrestle with fear. I do. But my dreams are winning out as my horizons expand faster than I can keep up with them.

There isn't any false bravado for me to say I am a much better preacher and minister than I ever was before. I know I'm helping people through my own experience of pain that I would have never reached before. That I am even preaching again is evidence of God's continued interest in my life.

Consequently, my values are different. My humanity is different. My audience has grown, and more than ever, I have something I am compelled to do and share.

Let your heart be open to the move of God. We can dream again.

GOING DEEPER

Read Genesis 37:1–11

1. Do you dream often? What kind of dreams do you have? Daydreams?

2. Have you ever had a dream so vivid that when you woke up, you were uncertain if it was real or not? Do your dreams motivate you?

3. When or how have your dreams come true? Where or how have your dreams been destroyed?

4. Sometimes great loss creates a fear of the future. Are you afraid of dreaming for the future? Why? How can you learn to dream again?

5. What role does faith or trust in God play in your dreams, ambitions, and goals?

Chapter 10

THE DARLING OF JERICHO

Then Joshua son of Nun secretly sent two spies from Shittim. "Go, look over the land," he said, "especially Jericho." So they went and entered the house of a prostitute named Rahab and stayed there. . . .

"Now then, please swear to me by the LORD that you will show kindness to my family, because I have shown kindness to you. Give me a sure sign that you will spare the lives of my father and mother, my brothers and sisters, and all who belong to them—and that you will save us from death." —Joshua 2:1, 12–13

Rahab? A chapter on Rahab? Really? Yes, Rahab. The King James Version uses an old-fashioned word to describe her: a harlot. More modern versions of the Bible simply call her a prostitute. The meaning doesn't escape you unless you're in the first grade, and nowadays I'd be tempted to doubt even that. In my world, calling a woman a harlot or a prostitute is not very nice at all. In fact, it might get you slapped, or worse.

To call a woman one of these ugly terms is to judge her for being promiscuous. It means she is loose. She is devoid of moral purity. She is the kind of girl Bible-believing, God-fearing mama's don't want their boys to hang out with. And if your upbringing is anything like mine, you may be able to imagine your mom wagging her finger while quoting the apostle Paul from 1 Corinthians 15:33, "Do not be misled: 'Bad company corrupts good character.'"

Harlots are not harlots all by themselves. Maybe you are one of those people who think those women are making a choice. I'll grant you, it is a choice, and maybe not even one of their own making. Just know this: however a woman came to be in this profession, most likely a horrific story lies behind it. It is more than safe to say that women don't choose this as a career path because it is what they always dreamed of doing. Generally some layer of coercion is involved and maybe even at the highest levels of government. Have you ever wondered why the king of Jericho knew the spies were at Rahab's house?

Whatever degree of manipulation is involved (and I would argue for the highest degree possible), there is a very real pain involved in the business of prostitution, not the least of which is the loss of human dignity. I titled this chapter "The Darling of Jericho," and there is a good reason to do so. Rahab was somebody's daughter, sister, granddaughter, aunt, niece, or friend. Somebody called her *darling*. She was loved, valued, and appreciated. On the other hand, she was somebody else's *darling*, and that meant she was used, abused, and once completely broken, discarded on the trash heap of life.

The kind of guys who make use of harlots are guilty of lasciviousness at the very least. That's another King James word you don't hear every day. There are certainly worse things you could say about guys like that. And since we can, let's do it.

Men who would use a woman who works at what Rudyard Kipling called the world's oldest profession have lost their own moral compass. Worse, they are completely willing to take advantage of another human for the sole purpose of gratifying their own base urges. And, guys, to turn a woman into an object is to undermine the value given her at creation. From there, it is only a small step from objectifying her to using and discarding her.

So here's Rahab. In the eyes of the world, she is T-R-O-U-B-L-E. Trouble. She is disease. She is heartache. She is ruin. And in most scenarios you could ever envision, nothing good could come from a liaison with her. Surely you know the type often characterized on the big screen. Big red lips. Outlandish clothes. Bereft of normal societal values. She is hard, harsh, calculating, cold, and often excruciatingly beautiful. But the truth is, descriptions or visualizations like that are nothing more than an embellished caricature designed to strip away the awareness of whatever human goodness remains.

While Hollywood sensationalizes promiscuity, the reality is far different. Rahab was a woman just like any woman today. We may not know everything about her, but trust me on this: she had a family, and with that family came a whole host of hopes, dreams, worries, fears, goals, daydreams, and wishes. And like most women, past and present, she faced the daily struggle of holding it all together and making it all happen. Can you at least entertain the probability that she didn't start out her life with the goal of being known far and wide and throughout history as Rahab the harlot?

It would be a huge mistake for us to deny her humanity by only seeing her through one set of scandalous parameters. We need to consider the full context of her life. It would be foolish to rush to judgment while forgetting that we share her humanity. Most importantly, it would absolutely be a major failure on our part not to recognize that she shared the same God-given possibilities that are in all of us.

Joshua 6 tells the story of the conquest of Jericho and how the walls came tumbling down. Considering God's command to destroy those nations completely (Deut. 7:2), verses 22–25 in Joshua 6 are simply astounding:

> Joshua said to the two men who had spied out the land, "Go into the prostitute's house and bring her out and all who belong to her, in accordance with your oath to her." So the young men who had done the spying went in and brought out Rahab, her father and mother, her brothers and sisters and all who belonged to her. They brought out her entire family and put them in a place outside the camp of Israel.
>
> Then they burned the whole city and everything in it, but they put the silver and gold and the articles of bronze and iron into the treasury of the LORD's house. But Joshua spared Rahab the prostitute, with her family and all who belonged to her, because she hid the men Joshua had sent as spies to Jericho—and she lives among the Israelites to this day.

That last phrase, "And she lives among the Israelites to this day," is absolutely amazing.

This is Rahab.

The harlot.

The lady of the evening.

The woman of ill-repute.

This is Rahab, the pagan, non-Jewish woman who had absolutely no part or parcel among the children of Israel. This is Rahab, who changed everything with this good confession: "The LORD your God is God in heaven above and on earth below" (Josh. 2:11).

When you hear those words from Rahab, you find some of the greatest hope ever. Even a cursory glance leads us to an extraordinary woman given the occasion to reach her full potential as a God-fearing follower. Rahab is given more than just a place of refuge; she is given the opportunity to find redemption. And with her redemption, she is afforded a restoration of value and worth. Because of her redemption and restoration, she is reconciled and brought fully into a community of faith!

"And she lives in Israel to this day" (Josh. 6:25).

Indeed.

I find this story simply amazing. While it's a story that ends well, it is not a story that ends there. In the great genealogy of Jesus, Matthew records her place: "Salmon the father of Boaz, whose mother was Rahab, Boaz the father of Obed, whose mother was Ruth, Obed the father of Jesse, and Jesse the father of King David" (1:5–6). Nobody will ever mistake me for the science guy—all the ins and outs of DNA elude me. But this is a simple thing all of us can understand. When Jesus was born, he had within him the genetic markers of Rahab. From the brothel to the manger, we find one of the greatest redemption stories of all time.

This is *my* hope. No matter how broken I am by my own sin and the sins of others, there is room at the table for me. That God would welcome Rahab means God still welcomes me!

Redemption is still found.

Restoration is still given.

Reconciliation is still to be had.

GOING DEEPER

Read Joshua 2:1–24; 6:1–27

1. What is predominant in Rahab's character? Would you consider her an opportunist? Or, do you see in her an incipient faith?

2. How does Rahab's occupation color your view of her? Should you see her that way or not?

3. In many respects, people like Rahab are considered taboo or unworthy. Where do you see pariahs in your community? Are you missing opportunities to include them in God's kingdom?

4. Are there areas or parts of your life that might be considered taboo? Does the story of Rahab give you hope? How?

5. What does knowing that Rahab is included in the genealogy of Jesus tell you about God? What does it say about the gospel?

Chapter 11

FLEECED

The angel of the LORD came and sat down under the oak in Ophrah that belonged to Joash the Abiezrite, where his son Gideon was threshing wheat in a winepress to keep it from the Midianites. When the angel of the LORD appeared to Gideon, he said, "The LORD is with you, mighty warrior."

"Pardon me, my lord," Gideon replied, "but if the LORD is with us, why has all this happened to us? Where are all his wonders that our ancestors told us about when they said, 'Did not the LORD bring us up out of Egypt?' But now the LORD has abandoned us and given us into the hand of Midian." —Judges 6:11–13

Once upon a time in a land not so far away, bad things happened. They hurt; I cried. They still hurt; I still cry. None of that was or is the end of the story. But pain is pain and struggle is struggle, and whether we're groaning in the grip of heartache and pain or basking amid sunshine and blue skies, understanding God can be really difficult. I know that's bound to sound outlandish or even heretical at first blush. But the truth is, before I experienced tragedy, I had absolutely no real idea of who God was and what God did.

Now don't get me wrong. I could quote Scripture and expound on doctrine. I could go toe-to-toe with anybody about what I believed the Bible to say. And I could preach—there was a time when I had a whole lot more self-confidence, and I absolutely loved every opportunity to preach. My whole identity was wrapped up in God and serving his people.

But there is a reason Satan is called the father of lies, and most of us have fallen for his two-pronged scam. I know I did. Most of us have been easy marks, and when Satan (or anybody he is using) says we are stupid, we believe him. When Satan says we are no good, we don't even argue. When Satan says we are worthless, we accept his words as the unvarnished truth.

How quickly we forget that each of us is made in the image of God. Within each of us resides something of the divine. Within all of us you can find something of intrinsic value and worth. As the old saying goes, "God don't make no junk!"

But questioning our value has never been Satan's end-game, so he ups the ante and raises the con—he takes deception to a whole new level. In the process, we have been hoodwinked, bamboozled, duped, hoaxed, and swindled. We've been suckered, fooled, taken for a ride, and fleeced.

How does he do this? Satan knows he can only go so far in making us doubt ourselves, so once he has accomplished that with some regularity, the next step is to have us reach the crazy conclusion that God is formed in *our* image—that somehow, someway we can make God fit our mold. That somehow, someway, we can manipulate the very essence that makes him God.

Take Gideon, for example. In Judges 6, Israel is in the punishment phase of a long cycle of disobedience, punishment, and deliverance. When the Angel of the Lord appears, he finds Gideon not standing up to his Midianite oppressors, but hiding food from them. Obviously, this is a time of heartache and despair for Gideon and his family. Nobody I know is suggesting that Gideon is a weakling or a wimp. Nobody thinks badly of him for trying to provide for his family.

But I suspect it comes as a complete surprise to all of us when an angel appears to Gideon and says, "The LORD is with you, mighty warrior" (Judg. 6:12). Gideon doesn't look or act like a mighty warrior, so maybe you can imagine with me that Gideon did the whole "who me?" thing. But *in fact*, Gideon never even reacts to being called a warrior. Instead, because he feels abandoned, he reacts to the idea of God being with him. And the truth is, he and the Israelites were suffering through the consequences of their own failures.

Sound familiar? It should. All of us understand the nature of consequences. But what is surprising is what comes in the next verse. The angel of the Lord tells Gideon, "Go in the strength you have."

Again, we get the "who me?" thing. Strength? What strength? If I can put words in his mouth, Gideon might well have said, "You want me to do your job, God?" Worse, he says, "My family is the weakest and I am the youngest" (Judg. 6:15).

Talk about great expectations! Just like that, Gideon has done what we all do. He has built two boxes. The first box contained the God who was somehow powerless, ineffectual, or unwilling to make a difference or meet a need. In the second box, Gideon found himself trapped by believing the lies of Satan about his lack of value and self-worth. After all, the God who fails or refuses to do what we want simply piles on more validation of our own unworthiness.

God's not big enough, and you're not worthy enough. As we vacillate between two such ugly extremes, Satan has us ever building boxes. Sometimes bigger, sometimes smaller, still we build. In our self-doubt and angst, we try to fit God into a box sized by whatever our current understanding of God might be. When he does big things, we build bigger boxes. When he doesn't do what we expect, we downsize. We have fallen for Satan's scam—hook, line, and sinker.

Now watch Gideon carefully. You'll have to read some of this on your own time—but you'll find that he is not unwilling to expand his God-box, so he asks for a sign to justify pushing out its walls a bit further. And as the story tells us, God gives him exactly what he wants.

At that point, Gideon is encouraged. He is even willing to do a little work for God. He is willing at least to entertain the idea that he can accomplish something. He is still afraid and uncertain of his value, but he expands his box with temporary walls, because who knows if God is really going to help him be big enough to fill it? But God is willing, and Gideon gets stretched even more. He learns that he is going to go out and fight a full-fledged war. Listen to Gideon's response:

> Gideon said to God, "If you will save Israel by my hand as you have promised—look, I will place a wool fleece on the threshing floor. If there is dew only on the fleece and all the ground is dry, then I will know that you will save Israel by my hand, as you said." And that is what happened. Gideon rose early the next day; he squeezed the fleece and wrung out the dew—a bowlful of water.
>
> Then Gideon said to God, "Do not be angry with me. Let me make just one more request. Allow me one more test with the fleece, but this time make the fleece dry and let the ground be covered with dew." That night God did so. Only the fleece was dry; all the ground was covered with dew. (Judg. 6:36–40)

I am not much of a carpenter, but Gideon must have been. He understood the adage about measuring twice before you cut. Gideon was using his fleece as a measuring stick to see just how big God's box was going to be. I don't know how big the box would have been, but in the next chapter we find that it wouldn't have been big enough. In Judges 7, God has Gideon whittle his army down to just three hundred warriors armed only with a pitcher, a trumpet, and a torch. I suspect you know the rest of the story. By Judges 8, we read that Gideon routed the entire Midianite army. But if we really want to know what happened, we need to go back to what the angel of the Lord said in the first place: "Go in the strength you have!"

Therein lies the rub. God says go in the strength *you* have. And *I* did. For much of my life, at my deepest level, it was all about me. What I accomplished, I did through strength of will and whatever expertise I could muster. I could give lip service to giving God credit, but that's all it was. I believed in God, but mostly I believed in me. Trapped by the lies of Satan, I was all too willing to believe them myself.

And it's crazy as I look back. It's amazing to me how deluded I was. It was at least eighteen months after my tragedy before I began to get the full measure of how broken I was. I was married again, Becki and I had embarked on a new career selling real estate together, and we were enjoying our new family to the fullest. What could be wrong with that picture?

No matter how confident I appeared on the outside, God was at best just an abstract figure I paid reluctant homage to. As it turns out, there were serious cracks that went deeper than our façade. Eventually I could not escape our real condition. We were broke, and our prospects were dim. I don't know how many job applications I filled out. I will never, ever forget the humiliation of putting all our kids on Medicaid while applying for and receiving food stamps. The more I tried to make life be about me, the deeper into despair I went. God had my attention, and as desperately as

I needed and wanted his help, I fought him every step of the way. Stubborn to the end.

The analogy I have used is building a box. Even after his victories, Gideon still tries to make God fit his box, his understanding. Check out Judges 8 where Gideon fashions a gold ephod. The text says, "All Israel prostituted themselves by worshiping it there, and it became a snare to Gideon and his family" (8:27).

As for Gideon, so for us. Building our boxes, limiting God, depending on ourselves is a snare. Worse, it is a recipe for failure. It took becoming a thoroughly broken man for me to get that. And even then, I resisted. Even now, I fight the temptation to see my successes and abilities as something I have forged out of trauma. But it's never about our strength or ability. It is always about God. He is the only real strength we have.

So if you are looking for a revival, if you are looking for redemption, it won't be found in a box of your making.

Put your hammer down.

Let go of the power drill.

Leave the saw alone.

Quit buying glue, nails, and screws—quit building boxes!

The strength you have is not your own; God is bigger than you imagine. It has been my experience that when I quit making everything about me, God shows up. Revival begins. Redemption happens. Stories change.

Mine did.

Yours can too.

GOING DEEPER

Read Judges 6

1. How do you personally define, describe, or explain oppression?

2. Based on your experience or knowledge of oppression, what brings it to an end?

3. Why do you think God called Gideon? Have you ever sensed God's call in your life? How did you respond? Did you attempt to test God?

4. Is there a place or purpose where you are resisting God's Spirit or calling? Do you try to contain God in a box of your own choosing?

5. What does the story of Gideon's fleece say to you? Are you prepared to be a Mighty Warrior?

Chapter 12

STUPID SAMSON

*Samson went down to Timnah and saw there a young Philistine woman.
When he returned, he said to his father and mother, "I have seen a
Philistine woman in Timnah; now get her for me as my wife."*

*His father and mother replied, "Isn't there an acceptable woman
among your relatives or among all our people? Must you go to the
uncircumcised Philistines to get a wife?"*

*But Samson said to his father, "Get her for me. She's the right one
for me."* —Judges 14:1–3

When my son Cole turned sixteen, he made one request: "I want
a girlfriend. Get me one." We laughed then; I still smile at the
memory. It was perfect Cole and indicative both of his funny,
demanding ways and his trust in us. Unfortunately for him, it was
a request we were unable to fill. And that reminds me of Samson.

Cole had other Samson-like attributes. Particularly his
Popeye-like biceps (his "guns," as he liked to say) and the six-pack
abdomen he was so proud of. If you were physically disabled and
had legs like sticks, you'd brag on your upper-body strength too.

Samson's story is quite funny to me and reminiscent of Cole.
It's hard to fathom somebody in our culture having Samson's
kind of conversation with our parents about the woman he might
want to marry. In fact, as much as I love my mother and father,

I would never have wanted them involved in my efforts to get a girl. After all, my mother was the mom who always managed to let the girl I was dating hear her tell me to make sure we kept a Bible between us.

Yes, that was my mom. And yes, I was that guy. Funny how she never said that again when I asked in return, "Can I just use a New Testament and turn it edgeways up?"

I digress.

Maybe you are not familiar with the account of Samson. His story begins with a woman who was unable to conceive. And in that agony, God intervened with the promise of a child. This promise came with an important condition: he would be dedicated to God with a Nazirite vow. Numbers 6 tells us much more about this vow, but to make it short and sweet, a person living this vow would be consecrated to God through a holy lifestyle. Sometimes the vow was taken for a brief period. Samson's was life-long

To Manoah and his wife, a child was born. His mother named him Samson. Judges 13:24–25 says, "He grew and the LORD blessed him, and the Spirit of the LORD began to stir him while he was in Mahaneh Dan, between Zorah and Eshtaol." By Judges 14, Samson's life takes a strange turn in the wrong direction—a turn that I am not sure was ever fully corrected.

He wanted what he wanted and didn't much care whether it was a smart choice or a smart direction. In fact, his decision-making process at this point justifies the name Stupid Samson. And it wouldn't be the last time. One needs only to add water, lather, rinse, and repeat.

Obviously being disobedient to his parents and to God was, and still is, a big no-no. But Samson's problems were compounded by many other character flaws.

Arrogance.

Pride.

Stubbornness.

Self-centeredness.

Narcissism.

Vainglory (that's a word we don't use much these days).

Unhealthy desires.

Now, I am not Samson with his bulging biceps, chiseled features, and flowing locks. I may not be the ugliest guy around, but I am not the one ladies swoon over. Still, I am Samson. I have such a robust desire to be strong, bold, confident, and assured. But often I am the exact opposite.

I really am Samson. Not infrequently (as I mentioned in the previous chapter) exercising my own strength is the leading cause of the big messes I tend to make. And even though deep down inside I know the ugly truth, I am self-deluded and infatuated with the pretend me. (Wanna see my guns?) I am proud of my presumed abilities. I am delighted by my assumed strength. I am Samson. Give me enough slack, and I can make a huge mess out of anything.

So here's Samson. Here's a guy who was desperately wanted. Here's a guy who was an answer to a mother's prayers. Here's a guy who came from God with specific instructions for both parents and child to follow. All of that to say, here's a guy who was dedicated to God at birth. You'd like to think that would mean something, wouldn't you? You'd like to think that this whole special situation would somehow play out in spectacular ways. And by the end of the story we do get spectacular, but Samson sure took a difficult road to get there.

You couldn't find a much worse example of a life lived far short of expectations. He married a Philistine—one of the biggest no-no's for Israel. We find him cavorting with a prostitute in Gaza (Judg. 16:1). And then there was the love of his life, Delilah. The Bible doesn't give any indication that the love was reciprocal. Far from it. At any rate, she was seemingly quite open to the temptation of bribery and betrayal. And just like that, how far the mighty can fall—especially from the holiness that supposedly marked his entire reason for existence.

One might wonder about Samson's proclivities. One might question his mental condition. And, one might consider some unknown trauma that altered his perceptions of reality. But in the end, he truly is a tragic figure. Even though he was given back his power for a final moment of revenge, the amazing spectacle of his renewed strength was a sobering end to a life full of unfulfilled promise.

Poor Samson. Poor Samson indeed. But in this tragic story of heartache and sin, another horror is more heartbreaking, more insidious, and far more common to our lives than we might ever want to recognize.

Spiritually speaking, Samson was stupid. Let's go back to the story for a moment. When he finally fell to the wiles of Delilah, his secret was revealed and his power was destroyed. After she finished shaving his head, she awoke him. Here's how the book of Judges records Samson's reaction: "He awoke from his sleep and thought, 'I'll go out as before and shake myself free.' But he did not know that the LORD had left him" (Judg. 16:20). Can you imagine the shock? Can you imagine the pain of his defeat? Can you imagine his not knowing the Lord had left him?

I have made a lot of mistakes in my life. I make a lot of mistakes even now. Some of those mistakes are garden variety. But the most stupid mistake of all is either thinking you have God in your life or simply missing the fact that through your actions and attitudes the presence of God has quietly gone away.

Maybe you are uncomfortable with the idea of the Lord leaving. I get that. I also get that there is a sense in which God never disappears. He is always here. But like any relationship, my behavior not only can strain it, it can destroy it. How does that happen? What does a life without God look like? Your experience may be different, but when it is all parsed out, the absence of God is always ugly.

In the aftermath of my family tragedy, my life became extremely ugly. Full of anger, bitterness, more anger, more bitterness, and the world's worst bad attitude. My life descended into the kind of ugly no one wants to see. I pushed family and friends away. I found no joy in anything. Little if anything in my life was remotely redeemable.

At least that's what I thought, but I am Samson. No, I was never led to a temple to entertain my captors. But make no mistake, I was just like Samson. Blinded by my own pain, held captive by the lies of Satan, I spiraled deeper and deeper into an ugliness all my own. Your ugliness doesn't have to look remotely like mine, but ugly is ugly.

In a passage in which we are warned about a number of different things, the apostle Paul caps it off with a major thought: "Do not grieve the Holy Spirit of God, with whom you were sealed for the day of redemption" (Eph. 4:30). As Samson was set apart by his Nazirite vow, so too we are set apart and consecrated by the Holy Spirit. Don't be like Stupid Samson. Don't forget who you belong to. Don't let your ugly win the day.

Obviously, God is the answer to the ugliness of sin. But how do you see God when all you can feel is anger, bitterness, and despair?

A friend read the first iteration of this chapter and asked, "Where is the gospel?" He was right to ask, and I needed the reminder. As it turns out, the gospel would live and make its presence known through relationship. The gospel would be seen through the lives and love of those who would not give up on me. In time, the old hymn would ring true: "I was blind, but now I see."

Cherish your relationships (you may be the gospel for someone)—especially your relationship with God. And remember what Paul told Timothy: "But you, man of God, flee from all this, and pursue righteousness, godliness, faith, love, endurance and gentleness" (1 Tim. 6:11).

Don't be stupid. Don't depend on your own strength. Live for God. Make him your top priority. Pursue those things that will glorify him and him alone. Be prepared to listen.

I don't want to be stupid.

Do you?

GOING DEEPER

Read Judges 13–16

1. Samson was known for his strength. What was his true strength?

2. In the end, did Samson honor God with his life? Why did you reach that conclusion?

3. I call Samson "stupid." What do you think Samson's fatal flaw was? Is arrogance and pride a part of the picture?

4. How do arrogance and pride cause you difficulties with others? With God?

5. What was the real import of Samson's destruction of the Philistine temple?

6. Samson is obviously a man who struggles with self-control. What are some areas in your life where you struggle with self-control? How do arrogance and pride lead to a lack of perspective?

Chapter 13

YOU ARE THE MAN!

So David triumphed over the Philistine with a sling and a stone; without a sword in his hand he struck down the Philistine and killed him.

David ran and stood over him. He took hold of the Philistine's sword and drew it from the sheath. After he killed him, he cut off his head with the sword.

When the Philistines saw that their hero was dead, they turned and ran." —1 Samuel 17:50–51

As I write this, I am fifty-four years old and in the second of two back-to-back fitness boot camps. Monday through Thursday I am on the football fields of our local high school by 5:50 each morning. Apparently, I am a glutton for punishment. We run, lift weights, run with weights, run the football stands, do agility drills, push sleds, jump rope, lift more weights, do push-ups and crunches, more jumping jacks, run with parachutes tied to our backs, and perform an obscene amount of the Satan-designed exercise called a burpee. And we do lots of core exercises—particularly planks. Planks are the measure of a man, and often I am found lacking.

And we hurt. A lot. Still, I am out there four days a week. I am trying to lose weight, get off blood pressure meds, lose weight, look better, and feel good about myself. Unless the editors made an after-hours deletion, you read "lose weight" twice in the previous sentence. I wrote it that way on purpose. Yes, it's that important to me.

I still have a long way to go. I may never be as skinny as I want to be. My knees may not let me do all the things I'd like. But, I am after a designation that may only be awarded in my mind. Just once before I die, I want to be considered an elite athlete.

Just five minutes. Just give me five minutes of accolades.

As it turns out, I am a fierce competitor, if only with myself.

As a youngster, I played lots of sports badly. I was best at soccer, but my best left an awful lot to be desired. At this stage of my life, I have learned to love running. It clears my head, relieves my stress, and occasionally pays for my sins.

Did you know donuts were a sin? Yes, that's why I run. Along with chocolate cake, ice cream, hamburgers, and steaks. But as one of my coaches likes to say, you can't outrun or out-train a bad diet. But I try. I try so very hard.

So here I am. Occasionally if I squint just right in the mirror after a particularly good day working out, I like to tell myself something affirming and exciting. I look into the mirror and say, "I am the *man!*"

If you are a guy or hang around guys, you may have heard the following prideful discussion:

"I am the man!"

"No, I am the man!"

"Who's the man?"

"I am the man."

And so the argument goes. I am the man!

While that's a brag not reserved just for athletic achievement, it can also be considered good form in any real or imaginary competition. If, in fact, you are the man, then any area of capability or accomplishment is a prime trash-talking opportunity. If we conquer or dominate, we guys must brag and bury the rest in our ever-expanding expertise! One must never squander a chance to talk trash, especially if it is true.

After slaying the giant Goliath and coming back to his own battle lines with the adoration of cheering soldiers ringing in his ears, I wonder if David ever said, "I am the man!" Pardon my silly goofiness, but I can almost hear David channeling the future Jimmie Walker: "I'm dy-no-mite!"

Can you imagine with me that it would have been easy for David to get caught up in all his hype? After all, 1 Samuel 18:5 says, "Whatever mission Saul sent him on, David was so successful that Saul gave him a high rank in the army. This pleased all the troops, and Saul's officers as well." Can you consider just for a moment that all his accomplishments quite possibly gave David a big head? Can you maybe contemplate a David who began at some point to feel a bit invincible?

And then there is the story of David, Uriah, and Uriah's wife, Bathsheba. David has an illicit liaison with Bathsheba and she becomes pregnant. To hide their affair, David brings her husband home from war to give him the opportunity to have sex with his wife. Even if you have never read this story in 2 Samuel 11, I am sure you have no trouble understanding what David is trying to do. But the cover-up fails because Uriah's sense of honor won't let him seek comfort while his men are still in battle. Ultimately, David sends him back to war with his own death warrant in hand. It's a sad, sick story, and it looms large in David's life.

Maybe I am giving David's humanity too much grace, and maybe I am invoking too much speculation, but I cannot help but wonder if believing his own hype got in the way of decent, clear, moral, godly thinking. I cannot help but suspect that as he lived his life of privilege, David reveled too much in his special calling from God. Success, privilege, and calling became an open invitation for pride and a decided lack of humility. Add all that up and, before you know it, the rules that apply to everyone else are quite easily flaunted.

I find it quite easy to believe that when David, the man after God's own heart, gazed at and ultimately sought the forbidden bathing beauty Bathsheba, he did so as a guy who believed his own press. Unfortunately, pride, lust, adultery, and murder do not pave the road to happy fulfillment, no matter who you are, David included.

To help him understand his epic failure, the prophet Nathan comes to David and tells him the parable of a stingy, miserly rich man. In this story, the rich man is obligated to feed a traveler. Instead of using his own resources to prepare a meal, he slaughters the beloved family pet of a poor man, a small ewe lamb. As David hears this, he becomes furious with the man who would do such a heartless thing. But, his anger is misplaced, for the story simply illustrated the ugliness of his own actions. Nathan famously says to David, "You are the man!" (2 Sam. 12:7).

For much of his life, David could gladly claim, "I am the man!" And in this tragic instance, those words rang true. He was the man. And so David confessed, "I have sinned against the LORD." With that confession, he effectively acknowledged his own hubris.

"I am the man!"

Sound familiar? It should. David's words are the words of all. I am the man. My ego, pride, selfishness, and foolishness have all conspired to lead me into sin against the Lord. Over and over again, my sinful broken humanity keeps me saying with great regret, I have sinned against the Lord.

I am the man.

And so are you.

I am David.

You are David.

We are David.

You can look down your nose at David if you want to, and I'll understand. But here is my reality: I consistently find myself teetering on the edge of just one, single, life-altering moment of stupidity. I am almost always just one bad decision away from believing my own press and making a choice I can never take back.

1 Corinthians 10:12 says, "So, if you think you are standing firm, be careful that you don't fall!" Or as the King James says, "take heed lest you fall."

I have fallen. I will fall again. But here is the good news: In Jesus Christ, I am more than the sum of my mistakes, failures, sins, and epic disasters. Because Jesus was and is the ultimate Savior, a day will come when my value and worth will be seen completely in him.

Redeemed and made whole, you and I both will be able to say, I am the man!

What a glorious day that will be!

GOING DEEPER

Read 1 Samuel 17 and 2 Samuel 11:1–12:15

1. Why was David so successful at an early age? Should it have been an indicator of more success or future problems? Why?

2. Political scandals often involve illicit sex. Why do you think that is?

3. What made David's sin with Bathsheba so outrageous?

4. Do you find David's anger with the man in Nathan's story ironic? Why is it so easy to see the evil in a story while ignoring it in ourselves?

5. Nathan referred to David's sin as contempt for the Lord. Why would he refer to sin that way? Can you see any sin in your life and how it is contemptuous toward God?

Chapter 14

ELIJAH, THE ORIGINAL FLASH!

Elijah said, "As the LORD Almighty lives, whom I serve, I will surely present myself to Ahab today...."

So Ahab sent word throughout all Israel and assembled the prophets on Mount Carmel. Elijah went before the people and said, "How long will you waver between two opinions? If the LORD is God, follow him; but if Baal is God, follow him."

But the people said nothing. —1 Kings 18:15, 20–21

I realized the other day that I have in my repertoire of words a well-used, possibly shallow little phrase. It comes out in bulletin articles and newspaper columns. I hear myself saying it in sermons I preach and classes I teach. It is an innocuous expression meant to convey understanding, empathy, and connectedness. As I write and speak, I often say, "I get it." I say I get it, because I do. I get brokenness. I get faith struggles. I get fear and anxiety. I get temptation, etc., etc., *ad nauseam.* If I sound a bit like a broken record, it's because I get it. I suspect you do too. With apologies to all and especially my long-suffering editors (Sorry, Tom and Gene, I know not what I do) and the promise to find another way to say the same thing in the future, I get Elijah. I really do.

In some faith traditions, ministers talk about having a calling. To the best of my understanding, it is a specific moment when they know their role, purpose, and direction in life. And in some of these traditions, they even have a special ceremony signaling the "calling" of this servant to the Lord. I never had a calling that resembled anything like that. There was no special moment, no light shining down, no angelic chorus to mark a new chapter in life. There was no ceremony to signal the beginning of a life of ministry, and yet I knew. In fact, while I can offer you no empirical evidence to bolster my claim, I have always known.

In fact, from the time I was a small boy, I heard the words, "You are going to be a preacher one day." Timothy had his grandmother, Lois (1 Tim. 1:5). I had my grandmother, Lilly. It wasn't so much an expectation, but an assumption. Over the years, I have had reason to wonder if there was some strange prescience involved. Whatever the case, I have always known my calling. From that perspective, I get the prophets of old. I get the sense of duty. I get the fire in the bones and the passion in the belly. I get the purpose. I get the drive. I get Elijah.

Elijah appears on Israel's national stage during a time of extreme ugliness. Ahab was the king, and the infamous Jezebel was his queen. We read in 1 Kings 16:30 that Ahab "did more evil in the eyes of the LORD than any of those before him." While there is every indication that Ahab would have been completely evil on his own accord, the very next verse points to his marriage with Jezebel as a specific source of evil in his life and reign. Two verses after that, we are told that Ahab "did more to arouse the anger of the LORD, the God of Israel, than did all the kings of Israel before him" (16:33).

Into that maelstrom stepped Elijah. Had he been fearful and timid in his confrontation with Ahab, I would have readily identified with his response. But that's not what happened. Elijah never backed down from Ahab. He was forthright and direct. Thanks to Scripture, we get to listen in as Elijah speaks: "I have not made trouble for Israel. But you and your father's family have. You have abandoned the LORD's commands and have followed the Baals" (18:18).

Elijah's challenge to the prophets of Baal was a rousing success. With the destruction and loss of Baal's acolytes and attendants, Ahab was publicly chastised and Jezebel's influence was undermined. And then the Bible says: "The power of the LORD came on Elijah and, tucking his cloak into his belt, he ran ahead of Ahab all the way to Jezreel" (18:46).

Elijah might have been the original *Flash*. Regardless, he was God's man standing up for the Lord. For a minister, there is such great satisfaction in knowing you are doing the work of God. There is great vindication in seeing things work out in a way that brings honor and glory to God. (And if we are truthful, there is also great pleasure in whatever reflected glory we might accrue.) I imagine this is exactly how Elijah felt. I imagine there was a sense of accomplishment and relief. I don't know if Elijah strutted or not, but I would have. I am positive there were times when I did.

And then came the death threat. Jezebel was not one to be trifled with. She did not suffer being thwarted lightly. As 1 Kings 19:2 tells us, "Jezebel sent a messenger to Elijah to say, 'May the gods deal with me, be it ever so severely, if by this time tomorrow I do not make your life like that of one of them.'" The very next verse tells us Elijah laced up his running shoes and fled, sprinting for his life.

One minute he is in high cotton, and in the next he is in high motion. The fields are burning down around him. I know, it's getting highly redundant, but I can't seem to help myself: Yes, I get Elijah. I get him in spades. I get him because I have been there. There were times in my ministry when a successful program or plan was hindered by shallow thinking—or worse, destroyed by jealousy. But then, there is often no telling what people will be threatened by.

Church and ministry programs are one thing; lives are another level of importance altogether. Like Elijah, I too have been on the receiving end of a death threat. While I didn't die, others did. Important others, my flesh and blood. There is a difference here between Elijah and myself, but only in degree. When faced with death, Elijah ran. As the story continues in 1 Kings 19, Elijah prays to die before he goes to sleep under a tree. Maybe you can't imagine all the fear, stress, anxiety, and even depression Elijah must have faced. But I can. I can because, well, you know, I get Elijah.

Of course, there is much more to Elijah's story. I love the fact that after expressing his desire to die, an angel of the Lord came and ministered to him. And it was enough, at least for the next forty days or so. While there was nothing spectacular or awe-inducing over what was provided, Elijah was given the necessary food, rest, and encouragement to continue the journey. So he did.

Forty days later, Elijah enters a cave to sleep and God shows up with a question: "What are you doing here, Elijah?" (1 Kings 19:9). In those words, I hear the echo of any number of questions. "What are you afraid of, Elijah? Why do you doubt? Have you forgotten who I Am?" In Elijah's answer, we get a pretty solid confirmation that Elijah is missing the big picture: "I have been very zealous for the LORD God Almighty. The Israelites have rejected your covenant, torn down your altars, and put your prophets to death with the sword. I am the only one left, and now they are trying to kill me too" (19:10).

Have I mentioned the fact that I get Elijah? After Karen and Cole's murders, I ran, but not toward God. Angels of various stripes were all around me offering sustenance and love, but I pushed them away and ran even farther. I ran in anger. I ran in defeat. I never entered a deep, dark physical cave, but emotionally and spiritually, I might as well have.

I have done what you asked, God.

I have given all I can, Lord.

I have suffered enough, God.

I am all alone, Lord.

What about me?

Like Elijah. I was looking for a different experience of God. I wanted answers that thundered from the sky. I wanted to be able to direct God and give him marching orders. Better yet, I wanted God to know what I needed—that is, as I perceived my needs—and to act accordingly. What's the point of being God if you can't zap your enemies with a little fire and brimstone?

I suspect you know how the story goes. Elijah experiences a colossal wind, a massive earthquake, and a fierce fire, but God is not in them. And then comes a still, soft whisper with the very same question God asked before: "What are you doing here, Elijah?" (19:13). You can read the rest of the story on your own, but God has some specific things to say to Elijah. Allow me to paraphrase rather loosely what is found in the next few verses . . . "Elijah, I am still here. I am still in charge. You are not alone" (1 Kings 19:15–18).

The loudest thing you may ever hear is the quiet whisper of God to every Elijah: "You are not alone." Indeed, Psalm 34:18 says, "The LORD is close to the brokenhearted and saves those who are crushed in spirit." Even more graphic is the imagery of Jesus when he was faced with the heartache and grief of Lazarus's loved ones. Do you remember what John tells us? "Jesus wept" (John 11:35).

I am thankful God still whispers and that whisper still roars: I am not alone! And neither are you. I love what Paul tells us in 2 Corinthians 1:3–4, "Praise be to the God and Father of our Lord Jesus Christ, the Father of compassion and the God of all comfort, who comforts us in all our troubles, so that we can comfort those in any trouble with the comfort we ourselves receive from God."

Even prophets of old had to be led and had to be told: You are not alone!

We are not *alone!*

GOING DEEPER

Read 1 Kings 17–19

1. Elijah did many powerful things as God's prophet. Why did he doubt God's presence?

2. Have you ever felt as discouraged as Elijah? Why or why not?

3. What does his story reveal about you?

4. Do you ever find yourself taking credit where it belongs to others? To God?

5. How important is the message "You are not alone"? With those same words, can you help someone who is struggling?

Chapter 15

IN THE PRESENCE OF THE KING–CELEBRATE!

For a full 180 days he displayed the vast wealth of his kingdom and the splendor and glory of his majesty. When these days were over, the king gave a banquet, lasting seven days, in the enclosed garden of the king's palace, for all the people from the least to the greatest who were in the citadel of Susa....

Queen Vashti also gave a banquet for the women in the royal palace of King Xerxes. —Esther 1:4–9

If I started this chapter by saying I don't understand the story of Esther, you'd probably quit reading. Why read an author who admits he doesn't know what he's talking about? Therefore, I am not writing those words, but it has been a struggle to keep from it.

I love a good party. In fact, I'd like nothing better than to drift from one celebration to another, but there is always another obligation to meet. There is always another deadline. There is always another problem to solve. There will always be difficulties and struggles of some kind or another. Life just cannot be a never-ending party. Being an adult sure gets in the way of having fun. A constant party just isn't how life works for most of us. In the story of Esther, well, that's not how life worked either. In fact, although a party is thrown at the beginning of the written story, one would be hard-pressed to think it would end in celebration.

The back story of Esther begins with an exiled people. The nature of an exiled and a displaced people lends itself to becoming a story of racism and hatred. That is in large measure what we find here. This story further segues into a story of political power and upheaval, complete with some good old boys who appear to want to keep their women chafing under the thumb. It contains more than a hint of sexism and the objectifying of women. Is it surprising that there would also be ladies using their physical assets to get what they needed?

In short, the story of Esther is a human story filled with the actions, antics, and foibles of people who lived long ago but weren't any different from us. We don't have the time or the space here to delve deeply into all the pertinent aspects of Esther's story. But because you have already bought this book, I feel a little bit obligated to give you an extremely short version of the main events.

So here goes: The Persian king, a dude known to history as Xerxes but with the unenviable given name of Ahasuerus (henceforth and forever referred to as King Whatshisname) was married to Queen Vashti, who was a physically beautiful lady by all accounts. Together they threw a hugely lavish party that lasted a full week, with the standing orders being to serve as much wine as anybody wanted.

At some point, the king wanted his queen to strut her stuff for all his assembled officials and guests. Wine related? I have no idea. But whether it was or not, Queen Vashti declined the invitation and the party was over. At least for her. She was deposed, and that was that. Except then a law was passed that decreed all men should be the masters of their houses. (Don't get mad at me—I am not making this stuff up.)

The search soon was on for the new queen, and that's where Esther, the niece of Mordecai, comes into play. I am always surprised by how she is described in the story: "This young woman, who was also known as Esther, had a lovely figure and was beautiful. Mordecai had taken her as his own daughter when her father and mother died" (Esther 2:7).

As now, so it was then, we too easily assign value and worth based on physical appearance. But I digress. Sure enough, Esther won the Miss Persia Beauty Pageant and became the new queen.

Now we have a story shift. Enter the villain. King Whatshisname elevated a guy named Haman over all his other officials and decreed that all members of the royal staff should bow down to him. When Mordecai refused to bow, Haman became livid, discovered Mordecai's ethnicity, and concocted a plot to rid the kingdom of all Jews. Not knowing that his own queen was Jewish and related to Mordecai, King Whatshisname followed Haman's suggestion and decreed the destruction of the Jews throughout the empire.

So, while Darth Vader . . . uh, I mean, while Haman and company celebrated, Mordecai, Esther, and their fellow-Jewish expatriates were confused and terrified. One day you are rocking along as the queen, and the next day you learn your life is forfeit. The Bible tells us that Mordecai tore his clothes, wore sackcloth and ashes, and mourned.

Because Esther was the queen, Mordecai knew she could possibly avert this tragedy in the making. But Esther was reluctant. To approach the king uninvited warranted a death sentence unless the king extended grace. Mordecai reminded her that being queen in the palace of the king was no guarantee of safety. Then, he uttered these famous words: "For if you remain silent at this time, relief and deliverance for the Jews will arise from another place, but you and your father's family will perish. And who knows but that you have come to your royal position for such a time as this?" (Esther 4:14).

To shorten the story of Esther and Mordecai—Haman continued to plot Mordecai's destruction while Esther worked quietly to thwart him. In the end, Haman realized he had overreached, the king was enraged at his murderous audacity, and our evil character met his Maker.

There are other important details. New laws were written allowing the Jews throughout the empire to seize their own futures by destroying their attackers. Better yet, on the heels of all this drama and death, the Jews were given every opportunity to live as productive citizens of their new land.

James Bond had nothing on the people of Mordecai and Esther. First given a license to kill, they were then given a license to party. Furthermore, this license had no expiration date:

> Because of everything written in this letter and because of what they had seen and what had happened to them, the Jews took it on themselves to establish the custom that they and their descendants and all who join them should without fail observe these two days every year, in the way prescribed and at the time appointed. These days should be remembered and observed in every generation by every family, and in every province and in every city. And these days of Purim should never fail to be celebrated by the Jews—nor should the memory of these days die out among their descendants. (Esther 9:26–28)

If you have never read the short saga of Esther, please take the time to soak it in. The truth is that this story looks and feels like one you could read on the front page of our newspapers. Except for the absence of a real-life king and queen, it sounds like our politics. It feels like our world. It echoes our own actions and attitudes. It is a story just as modern as it is ancient.

The Jews had every reason to celebrate. They had just been delivered from a death sentence. They entered a new world—one in which they were no longer strangers in a strange land but full-fledged citizens. It was a new day for them. How could they not throw a party?

What we need to realize is that we are just like them. Through Jesus, we have been invited to the ongoing, never-ending party of God. We are an imperfect people full of sin and facing destruction, but we've been invited to come as we are and join the celebration. Through the grace of God in the gift of Jesus, we can die to our sin, move beyond our failures, and live above our imperfections. Through Jesus, we are invited to the ongoing, never-ending party of God.

Think about it. In Revelation 21:5, Jesus said, "I am making everything new!" Even when you can't yet see it, even when your life is still stuck in the mud, the same Jesus still creates a new perspective. We sing about living in a world that is not our home, and we must decide if that is true. We must decide if we really want to live beyond our failures. Because if we do, we are right on the cusp of having the right perspective.

A party outlook.

A party attitude.

A party life.

A celebration perception.

Not certain of your invitation? In Chapter Three, we discussed Jesus's story of the prodigal son who ran off and lived a life of dissipation. But there's a little epilogue to that story that we did not address. After the wayward boy wises up and comes home, the father throws a party. Listen in: "But the father said to his servants, 'Quick! Bring the best robe and put it on him. Put a ring on his finger and sandals on his feet. Bring the fattened calf and kill it. Let's have a feast and celebrate. For this son of mine was dead and is alive again; he was lost and is found.' So they began to celebrate" (Luke 15:22–24).

The story of Esther, Mordecai, and those ancient Jews is our story. If it doesn't feel like it at this moment, well, I understand. When you are hurting, parties are hard to handle. When you are grieving, celebrations are hard to take. In fact, in the aftermath of our calamity, I found it easy to be angry at the joy of others. In that respect, I was awfully like the elder brother in the prodigal son story. If that's where you are, then allow me to give you a bit of advice: First, try as hard as you can to not rain on the parade of others. Second, do remember the most famous words of Mom: "If you can't say anything nice, don't say anything at all!" Inflicting your pain on others will not lessen the pain you feel.

It may take a while for you to get there, and that's okay. Just remember, we share in the celebration of God—but only if we come to the party!

Are you in the presence of the King?

GOING DEEPER

Read the book of Esther and Luke 15

1. What are the similarities between the story of Esther and that of the prodigal son?

2. What is important about the similarities?

3. What do Haman and the older brother have in common?

4. What character in either story do you identify with most? Why?

5. How has God prepared you? For what? Is there something you should be doing now?

Chapter 16

DANNY AND THE THREE FIREMEN

Shadrach, Meshach and Abednego replied to him, "King Nebuchadnezzar, we do not need to defend ourselves before you in this matter. If we are thrown into the blazing furnace, the God we serve is able to deliver us from it, and he will deliver us from Your Majesty's hand. But even if he does not, we want you to know, Your Majesty, that we will not serve your gods or worship the image of gold you have set up."
—Daniel 3:16–18

The Partridge family. Just knowing the name dates me. That I write it in a book may mean you ignore me for being too dated to be relevant. But how I loved watching the Partridge family! Susan Dey was beautiful. The music (I owned the albums) was fantastic. I wanted to be David Cassidy.

In the height of Partridge family mania, I asked my father if I could wear my hair just like David Cassidy. That was bad timing on my part. We were fully engaged in the culture versus religion wars over the length of a man's hair. Maybe you remember that time. Maybe you remember the verse often cited: "Does not the very nature of things teach you that if a man has long hair, it is a disgrace to him?" (1 Cor. 11:14).

Not to be deterred by what I saw as a faulty definition of the word "long," my next question was, if not David Cassidy, could I wear my hair the length of Danny Bonaduce's? Danny Bonaduce was the red-haired drummer of the bunch. His hair was long, but not the epic length of David's. That length would have been acceptable to me, but only by a hair.

Okay, I get it. This is ancient history and not current pop culture we are talking about. On the other hand, have you ever heard of the truly ancient group Danny and the Three Firemen? Their harmony with God was simply astounding. You probably know them better as Daniel, Shadrach, Meshach, and Abednego.

Described as perfect physical specimens, they are handsome, gifted, smart, and swift on the uptake. No matter how you try to parse it, these guys were the total package with an added upgrade. If you don't believe me, check out the scripture that says the king "found them ten times better than all the magicians and enchanters in his whole kingdom" (Dan. 1:20).

Talk about landing on your feet! Unfortunately, success often breeds jealousy and contempt. All four of these young men would face a test. In the crucible, they would have to decide who they truly served. Most likely you know the stories. The three we call Shadrach, Meshach, and Abednego got caught between a law and a hot place—a law they couldn't follow and people who would not be satisfied until they did. Their refusal to bow the knee was met with all the fury King Nebuchadnezzar could summon. Into the blazing fiery furnace they went, a furnace so hot that the flames killed the men who threw them in. And yet they survived under the protection of God, unhurt, unsinged, and without even the smell of smoke permeating their clothes. Who couldn't serve a God like that?

Then there is the other story of jealousy and contempt. This time it is Daniel's turn in the spotlight—or the lion's den. The spotlight was big and bright and brought on its share of trouble. According to Daniel 6, King Darius appointed 120 provincial governors to rule over his kingdom with three administrators to oversee them. Daniel was one of the three. Did I mention the spotlight was big and bright? Yes, it was, and it was going to get brighter. Daniel's job performance was such that he was soon promoted over the entire kingdom. Because he was in such a prominent role, somebody else wasn't. Accordingly, somebody (or somebodies) was jealous.

After failing to find anything corrupt to use against him, these envious people conspired in a devious way to undermine Daniel in the eyes of the king. They convinced Darius to enact a law that called for a thirty-day halt to all prayers to anyone other than the king.

Daniel, being a God-fearer, continued his life of prayer. This made him easy fodder for the jealous co-conspirators. They found him in prayer and wasted little time before informing the king and reminding him of the decreed punishment for disobedience. And, as the story goes, Darius was not pleased with the quandary he was in and sought diligently for some way to save Daniel. But, because the law of the land said no edict of the king could be changed, Darius was stuck. And Daniel? Daniel was headed to the lion's den!

After the king had Daniel tossed, he endured a long, sleepless night. When morning broke, the king anxiously found himself at the entrance to the lion's lair, hoping against hope that Daniel had been spared. And he was. According to Scripture, there wasn't a mark to be found on Daniel.

Whether it is Shadrach, Meshach, and Abednego or Daniel, these stories are vivid and compelling. Both are exciting, thrilling, and inspiring. Both show good men doing the right thing. Both report rewards at the end. Both stories are powerful and positive examples of what it means and how it looks to follow God.

Still, I struggle with them. I read stories like these and wonder what's wrong with me. Why was I not worthy? Why was I not delivered? Why them? Why not me? Maybe you can relate.

One time I went to the doctor because I couldn't turn my head. My neck was painfully stiff and nothing would relieve it. After a thorough examination, the doctor asked if I had any stress, and of course, I said no. No stress, no worries, no problems. At that point, he asked some probing questions about my life. The most immediate thing on my mind was Cole's very recent diagnosis. We had been told he had a life expectancy of only a few more years. When I relayed that to the doctor, he laughed. Not because it was funny, but because I claimed to have no stress.

So when I say maybe you can relate, I know and you know the truth: Yes, you can!

What about my time in the fiery furnace? What about your time in the lion's den? When you or I look at our own life experiences, we see that some of them have been bitter, horrid, ugly affairs, and God didn't stop the burn; God didn't shut the mouths of the lions. My, what sharp teeth they have!

We know that fiery furnaces and lion's dens come in every shape and size imaginable. We know that even when the lions are not hungry, they still like to nip at our heels. We know long before we fall into the fiery furnace that some are extremely busy stoking the fires.

God delivered Shadrach, Meshach, and Abednego.

God delivered Daniel.

Why won't God deliver me? He didn't.

He didn't save you either from the sharp critical tongues of the people you are supposed to trust. He didn't save you from your epic failures. He didn't save you from things out of your control. He didn't save you from the hands of evil people. I get all of that.

Have you ever wondered what it would be like to be saved like Danny and the Three Firemen? I confess that I have. Do you remember what Shadrach, Meshach, and Abednego told the king when faced with the prospect of being turned into crispy critters? They said, "If we are thrown into the blazing furnace, the God we serve is able to deliver us from it, and he will deliver us from Your Majesty's hand. But even if he does not, we want you to know, Your Majesty, that we will not serve your gods or worship the image of gold you have set up" (Dan. 3:17–18).

Why did God save Danny and the Three Firemen? I don't know. I could surmise that God did it to show his power, to prove who he is. That's as good an answer as any. The real question isn't why he did or why he didn't. The real question is, Will we serve him anyway? The real question is, Will we trust him?

Another confession: That's not what I want to write. That's not what I want to say. I'd rather have a definitive answer. I'd rather know that whatever comes, God is going to save me.

And he did. Not like I imagined. Not like I wanted. Not like I sometimes demand. As much as I fight against it, this world is not my home. What happens here is not the end. Salvation belongs to our God. I am reminded of what John recorded in Revelation 7:10–12:

> They cried out in a loud voice: "Salvation belongs to our God, who sits on the throne, and to the Lamb."
>
> All the angels were standing around the throne and around the elders and the four living creatures. They fell down on their faces before the throne and worshiped God, saying: "Amen! Praise and glory and wisdom and thanks and honor and power and strength be to our God for ever and ever. Amen!"

It has not been easy. In fact, it is often still hard to accept the answers I have found. It is still difficult to trust at times. Bluntly speaking, as I started writing this book years ago, I never thought I could get to the place of speaking like Job: "Though he slay me, yet will I hope in him" (13:15).

But here I am.

I'm still standing.

You can stand too.

GOING DEEPER

Read Daniel 1 and 6

1. Has life ever thrown you curveballs? Were some of these difficulties the result of jealousy? How did you handle it?

2. How are the stories of Daniel and his three friends like the story of Jesus?

3. What does it mean to trust God? What does it mean to trust God in the middle of turmoil and trauma?

4. Have you ever been wrongly accused, suffered for it, and later vindicated? What does vindication call for in your response to those who hurt you?

5. Where do you need to give grace and forgiveness?

Chapter 17

MARY, DID YOU KNOW?

In the sixth month of Elizabeth's pregnancy, God sent the angel Gabriel to Nazareth, a town in Galilee, to a virgin pledged to be married to a man named Joseph, a descendant of David. The virgin's name was Mary. The angel went to her and said, "Greetings, you who are highly favored! The Lord is with you."

Mary was greatly troubled at his words and wondered what kind of greeting this might be. —Luke 1:26–29

I have traveled all over the world, courtesy of the United States Navy. I have transited both the Panama and Suez Canals. I have sailed around and through the fjords and glaciers of Chile in South America. I have visited island after island in the blue-green waters of the Caribbean. I have been to Africa. I have crossed the Atlantic and sailed the Mediterranean. I have gone below the equator. I have bought gold and pistachios in the souks of Bahrain. I have toured ancient Spanish cathedrals.

Like you, I have been privileged to view countless wonderful things in my life. I have seen the beauty of a woman standing to be my wife. I have held a newborn baby. I have watched children grow up and start families of their own. I have enjoyed holidays, vacations, anniversaries, and special meals too numerous to count.

On the other side of the coin, I have also experienced heartache. I know the searing pain of tragedy and loss. I have wept with others. I have sobbed for myself. I have left knee prints in the fresh dirt of a double grave. Years later I still find myself kneeling there from time to time.

Life is so full of varied and rich experiences from one extreme to another. In that vein, Forest Gump, philosopher extraordinaire, exquisitely once said, "Life is like a box of chocolates. You never know what you're gonna get." Indeed. If a box of chocolates can be compared to a lifetime of experiences, then the metaphor is quite apt. But of all the experiences we might have, whether expected or not, good or bad, fun or sad, nothing we might live or imagine can adequately compare to the experience of Mary, the mother of Jesus.

My impression of Mary isn't one of a cosmopolitan socialite. Mary isn't a noticeable member of a prominent family. Her life isn't lit in neon. She is not featured in the society section of the *Nazareth Gazette*. She hardly appears sophisticated.

One might more easily get the impression of a young, simple peasant girl. No one among the living today is certain of Mary's age when her life began to radically change. While modern tradition seems to like the idea of a young woman in her twenties, scholars and theologians alike believe Mary to be anywhere from twelve to sixteen years old.

With apologies to all the young ladies I have ever known in the age span of twelve to sixteen, I can't think of one who would be mentally, emotionally, and spiritually prepared to become the mother of the Savior of the world. That's heavy stuff, is it not? Can you imagine? I'm not so sure Mary could have been equipped either to imagine or dream such a thing.

Unfortunately, when I read the text, I almost want to laugh. Not because I disbelieve, and not because it isn't a serious passage of Scripture. I laugh, however awkwardly or inappropriately, because the text and dialogue seem so understated. After the greeting from the angel Gabriel, the Bible says Mary was deeply troubled by his initial remarks.

You think so? If it was you or me, I am convinced the text would rightly say that we were terrified and speechless beyond belief.

Think about it like this: Devotional art often portrays angels as cute fluffy creatures with beatific expressions of earnest human devotion. Where that wishful, fanciful thinking comes from, I'm not sure. My impression of angels is quite different. More times than not, when somebody encounters an angel in Scripture, that somebody experiences knee-rattling terror. Case in point: When the angel of the Lord appeared to the shepherds to announce Jesus's birth, Luke tells us, "They were terrified." So much so that this angel had to tell them, "Don't be afraid."

And Gabriel? I'd hate to meet him in a dark alley—or anywhere else for that matter. So back to the understated moment where Luke said Mary was greatly troubled. Really? You think so? Why else would Gabriel's next words be, "Do not be afraid, Mary, for you have found favor with God."

If I were Mary, I'd call for a thirty-minute break—most likely to change my clothes. How's that for an image you can't quite get out of your head? Nonetheless, Gabriel pushes on with his agenda. "Hey, Mary, quit hyperventilating already and get this: You are going to have a baby, and he will be called the Son of God!"

How Mary found the presence of mind to communicate that she was still a virgin is beyond me. And yet, the text clearly states she did. To make this even more amazing, she was somehow able to accept that God was at work in her life in ways incomprehensible.

It is a whole lot easier to read this story and accept it at face value without ever acknowledging Mary's humanity. I doubt I have even come close to doing her justice. Can you reach deep and agree that this was a unique moment in time for Mary? Can you recognize that there are more questions about her emotions and understanding than we will ever understand? I know this: when it comes to story time in heaven, I want to be there to hear her tell it.

I love the next part of this story; it gives me a bit more insight into her state of mind while also fitting in with the understated essence of it all. Gabriel leaves, and the very next two verses say, "At that time Mary got ready and hurried to a town in the hill country of Judea, where she entered Zechariah's home and greeted Elizabeth" (Luke 1:39–40).

At that time?

Hurried?

Are you prone to understatement much, Dr. Luke? I cannot prove it, but I have a sneaky suspicion that the text should have indicated something a little like Speedy Gonzales. Remember when Elijah ran ahead of Ahab's chariot? Now this is Mary pretending to be the Flash.

Let's be real. When the angel Gabriel shows up and announces you will become pregnant by the Holy Spirit and deliver a baby who will be called the Son of God, a leisurely Zip-a-Dee-Doo-Dah stroll out of town is not what follows.

No way.

And yet, in her humanity, Mary the mother of Jesus is a lesson of hope for all of us.

Fear and confusion are normal reactions in the mortal experience. So is needing reassurance and comfort. Mary found those things in her cousin Elizabeth's miraculous greeting. Better yet, even though she couldn't begin to know what the birth of her baby would mean in all its wondrous glory, the compiled evidence led her to a faith in a God who was bigger than her fear. So she sang,

> My soul glorifies the Lord
> and my spirit rejoices in God my Savior,

for he has been mindful
of the humble state of his servant.
From now on all generations will call me blessed,
for the Mighty One has done great things for me—
holy is his name.
His mercy extends to those who fear him,
from generation to generation.
He has performed mighty deeds with his arm;
he has scattered those who are proud in their
inmost thoughts.
He has brought down rulers from their thrones
but has lifted up the humble.
He has filled the hungry with good things
but has sent the rich away empty.
He has helped his servant Israel,
remembering to be merciful
to Abraham and his descendants forever,
just as he promised our ancestors. (Luke 1:46–55)

I have no idea what Mary thought in the days, weeks, and months to follow. I don't know what she understood. I cannot imagine that all was crystal clear to her. In fact, after Jesus was born and the shepherds made their appearance, Scripture says this: "But Mary treasured up all these things and pondered them in her heart" (Luke 2:19). I find great comfort in this simple verse. Here was Mary, the mother of Jesus, and she was just like us. She didn't have all the answers. She couldn't possibly know how the rest of her life would play out. She couldn't begin to understand what "Immanuel, God with us" would be like.

As Mark Lowry asks in the title of his highly popular song, "Mary, Did You Know?" Indeed, did you know all the things your son would do? Could you have imagined the miracles? Could you ever have thought for a moment that the dead would rise? Is there any way you could have remotely grasped that your child, born in a manger, announced by angels, was in fact, the Creator of the universe?

Mary, could you know? No, she didn't. She couldn't know. She couldn't possibly have understood all the ramifications this child would have in her life and the life of the world. She couldn't know, but she trusted God regardless.

Ahhh, Mary, you couldn't know. Your humility and vulnerability are just what I need to see. I am thankful for your experience. Your faith, trust, and ultimate acceptance are a profound example for me.

May each of us be blessed with the strength to hold on, wait, and trust in the Lord. He writes stories far better than we could ever imagine.

GOING DEEPER

Read Luke 1:26–56; 2:1–21

1. Do you think the popular conception of angels is accurate? Why or why not?

2. Put yourself in Mary's shoes; how would you have reacted to Gabriel the angel showing up? Fear? Disbelief?

3. Do you think Luke paints a true picture of how traumatic and confusing this episode might have been?

4. What do you think Mary meant by the words, "I am the Lord's servant"? Resignation? Faith? Trust?

5. In what ways can Mary be an example to you today?

Chapter 18

THE OTHER JOSEPH

Because Joseph her husband was faithful to the law, and yet did not want to expose her to public disgrace, he had in mind to divorce her quietly....

When Joseph woke up, he did what the angel of the Lord had commanded him and took Mary home as his wife. But he did not consummate their marriage until she gave birth to a son. And he gave him the name Jesus. —Matthew 1:19, 24–25

Jude Cole Ferguson. Doesn't that name just roll off your tongue like the finest bread pudding? Okay, so I crave bread pudding. It is my favorite dessert, and I'll only share it with you if I must.

That's kind of the way I feel about this first grandchild, the namesake of my deceased son Cole. Holding that baby boy is like holding a slice of heaven, and I don't want to share him with anybody. As clichéd as it might be, whoever first said "If I had known what having grandchildren was like, I would have skipped kids altogether" was absolutely on target. Some of you might not have a clue what I am talking about. A year ago, I was in exactly the same place. Don't worry. If it ever happens, you will understand perfectly.

Jude Cole Ferguson. Yes, I am looking for every opportunity to publicly let that name roll off my lips. But there is a funny little detail about my relationship with Jude Cole that he has no idea about. I assume that one day his dad will explain it to him, or maybe he'll find this dusty old book somewhere and recognize his grandfather's name. If he is bored, he'll read it and discover what I am about to divulge.

Jude Cole Ferguson (there's that name again) is not my biological grandson. I have zero connection with him as a blood relative. Zip. Zero. Nada. Nothing. That's because his father is not my biological child. We share not a single physical aspect—at least, not the kind that can be passed on through the baby-making process.

Being a father is an amazing thing. So is being a husband. After the deaths of Karen and Cole, I eventually reconnected with and married Becki. Years earlier we had dated seriously for four years. After we broke up, I joined the navy to get out of town, and eventually I got married and had my first family.

And now, with my new blended and blessed family, I have had the amazing experience of becoming a father in at least three ways. First by adoption (Kyle), then by birth (Cole and Conner), then by adoption once more (Casey), and finally, through marriage to Becki, I became a stepfather to two very special guys (Michael and Max).

Kyle, Cole, Conner, Michael, Max, and Casey. That's six boys. Read 'em and weep. No, really. Cry a little for me. I am way out of my league with all these dudes. All smart. All good looking. And all way more talented than me.

At any rate, I digress. All six young men came to me in different ways in different times. I love them all. I love them equally. How they got here is immaterial. One of the things I have learned through my family tragedy and subsequent remarriage is this: Sometimes you don't get to choose family. Sometimes family happens to you whether you are ready or not, whether you want it or not. I am thankful for family.

However it happens, family is family—and being family requires you to open yourself up in ways you might never have imagined before. We are accustomed to looking with wonder and awe at the life Mary was thrust into, and we should look with the same wonder at Joseph's suddenly changed life. If you believe, as I do, in the providence of God, then you most likely have already reached the same conclusion: God picked the right woman and the right man to be the earthly parents of Jesus.

Yes, there is much good in Joseph's story, much to admire and emulate. We can focus on his honorable outlook and desire to protect Mary's virtue. We can talk about his sense of justice and fair play. Whatever you do, don't limit how much we can know and grow from looking at the life of Joseph. I love his story. It is full of drama, suspense, heartache, loss, and all the touching moments of human devotion.

Here is a story of a father who has a special bond with a son. Unfortunately, with Herod's introduction, it is also a story of power, jealousy, and injustice. On the other hand, it becomes a story of redemption, grace, and being used by God.

You'd like to think that the birth of God-in-the-flesh would have had more fanfare. You'd like to think the birth of the Savior of the world would be free from drama, negativity, and plain old ugliness, but it's wasn't. Even though this is the story of God coming among us, it is still a human story, and unfortunately, we are human through and through.

So, while Jesus was "God in a bod," we mustn't forget or somehow miss the completely human element that played such a critical role in this story. You can look at Mary's miraculous pregnancy, and it was amazing. But other than an angel and a vision or two, nothing is miraculous about Joseph's side of the story. He didn't conceive; he had no role in the conception.

Joseph was just a guy. He wasn't superhuman. He wasn't a star. He was just a guy. Tell yourself that again: *Joseph was just a guy.* He was a man just like me. Flesh and blood, a product of his own environment, Joseph was just like any other man.

Dads, this means Joseph was just like you. Believe it or not, the proof is in the story. In fact, his initial thoughts about Mary's pregnancy lead me to conclude he was a man just like us. Admit it—you, too, would have cancelled the wedding to a fiancée who turned up pregnant. While Joseph wanted to do the right thing by her and had the inclination to deal with the situation using mercy and grace (hold on to the idea of mercy and grace, we'll get back to that in minute or two), he still wanted out.

Can you blame him or his humanity?

Don't point your finger at me. I am not blaming him, for sure. In fact, if I found out that I was going to be a father again, I'd surely be tempted to take a slow boat ride to the Bahamas—anything to get out of Dodge (unless Jude Cole was involved). So, hold on to Joseph's humanity for a bit, and let's give him a little credit for basic human goodness.

There are more than fair indications that Joseph was not only a decent guy, but also a good husband and father to Mary and Jesus. The Gospels don't supply as much detail as we might like, but consider these two short episodes:

When they had gone, an angel of the Lord appeared to Joseph in a dream. "Get up," he said, "take the child and his mother and escape to Egypt. Stay there until I tell you, for Herod is going to search for the child to kill him."

So he got up, took the child and his mother during the night and left for Egypt, where he stayed until the death of Herod. And so was fulfilled what the Lord had said through the prophet: "Out of Egypt I called my son." (Matthew 2:13–15)

And second, remember the story of twelve-year-old Jesus going missing on the family's return home from a Jerusalem Passover trip. When they found him, Mary exclaimed, "Son, why have you treated us like this? Your father and I have been anxiously searching for you" (Luke 2:48).

Obviously, the first story shows Joseph's willingness to listen to God and his willingness to protect his family. That's what good guys do to the best of their ability. But the second story adds layers of detail to our understanding of this man who would be the earthly father of Jesus. Notice that he is actively involved in providing Jesus with the right example of devotion to God and ensuring that his boy knows God's story—hence the Passover trip. That is all important, but the last verse is key: "And Jesus grew in wisdom and stature, and in favor with God and man" (Luke 2:52).

While skimpy on all the details, this one, small verse tells us that Jesus grew educationally, physically, socially, and in his relationship with God. With respect and admiration to all single parents, in an intact family bringing up children is not just a mom's job or a dad's job. It's the work of a father-mother combo.

I hope you see good stuff in the life of Joseph. I certainly do. In fact, when I look at all my failures and inadequacies as a husband and father, I know I can do better just by focusing on those basic things every family needs.

But there are two things about Joseph that can become game-changers in our families and church families. In fact, they would change just about every facet of our public lives, politics, and public discourse. They are the two things missing too often, the two things we need most (outside of God, but reflective of God). They are the best parts of Joseph's story.

We could talk about the importance of adoption, children, fatherhood, and so on. We could acknowledge that each child, made in the image of God, has his Father's DNA. Those are all important things. But what do I see in Joseph that is missing frequently from my life? Mercy and grace. I believe it was Joseph's inclination to mercy and grace that opened him up to be used by God.

Mercy and grace. So much of my life would be easier, so many of my actions as a husband and father would be different if they were filtered through a heart tempered by mercy and grace. When Paul tells fathers not to stir up anger in their children, that's what he is talking about (Eph. 6:4). When Peter reminds us that love covers a multitude of sins, that's what he is talking about (1 Pet. 4:8).

I want to be like Joseph. Yes, I want to provide for, care for, and protect my wife and children. I want to help them grow in all the important ways. I want to lead them to a vibrant relationship with God.

Regardless of what Joseph faced, immaterial to how he felt, irrespective of what he had to grow into, I see a man of mercy and grace. On my own, I am not that good. By myself, I am a disaster waiting to happen. Maybe too often a disaster happening. But because God, Mary, and Joseph did their thing, I can experience the Messiah. I can become a person of mercy and grace. I am not there yet, but God is still working on me (and using a precious grandson in the process).

How about you? Are you up for a little mercy and grace?

Here's a little advice:

Quit being so judgmental.

Let a smile crack your face.

Get in touch with the Spirit of God that fills you.

Show a little mercy and grace.

Forgive.

Be a blessing.

The world is still a beautiful place—act like you know it!

GOING DEEPER

Read Matthew 1:18–25; 2

1. Did Joseph have a right to be skeptical? Would you have been?

2. From Joseph's perspective, how hard would it be for you to believe Mary's story?

3. Do you think Joseph really understood what was happening? How much mercy and grace would you need to function in a story like this?

4. Joseph doesn't get much play. His fatherhood is overshadowed by the Fatherhood of God. How much credit do you think he deserves? Why?

5. From the brief accounts we have, it appears that Joseph fully embraced his role. Where or how do you need to embrace and grow in the roles or situations of your life? How is Joseph an example for you?

Chapter 19

THE LOCUST MAN

*As John's disciples were leaving, Jesus began to speak to the crowd
about John: "What did you go out into the wilderness to see? A reed
swayed by the wind? If not, what did you go out to see? A man dressed
in fine clothes? No, those who wear fine clothes are in kings' palaces.
Then what did you go out to see? A prophet? Yes, I tell you, and more
than a prophet." —Matthew 11:7–9*

At this stage of my life, I love being a preacher. I love speaking. I
love ministering. I love helping others come to know Jesus or grow
closer to him.

My tribe doesn't talk much about "being called" into ministry.
It is too touchy-feely for us. Even so, I knew at a young age that I
was supposed to be a preacher. I have memories of an older lady at
church when I was in second or third grade who told me repeatedly that I would be a preacher someday. And then there is my
grandmother, Lilly, whom I mentioned back in Chapter Fourteen.
She told me all through my preteen and teenage years the very
same thing.

Maybe it sounds like hyperbole to hear me say that I have
always known I was to be a preacher, but there it is. I knew when
speaking for the first time at Camp WAMAVA in the summer after
my third-grade year. I knew at the tender age of fifteen when I was

asked to speak weekly at the little African American Church of Christ on Gibson Road.

I knew when I started college, and when I joined the navy. I knew when I quit preaching in anger, pain, and frustration, and when I argued with my closest friends about my preaching viability. I knew when I filled in at a couple of area churches, and when I argued with Richard Brooks, one of my current elders, that I would not preach again and wasn't a candidate for their open ministry position.

I knew. I have always known that God and ministry had a hold on my life.

I knew.

Sometimes I dreamed of other things. Sometimes I wanted a job away from the demands of people who could be so hurtful and selfish. Sometimes I needed to be treated more fairly, to not struggle so hard financially. Sometimes I cried after meeting with the elders. Sometimes I lived in perpetual fear of being fired. And it is not as though I didn't see those things happen to others. It is not as though being a preacher was or is a walk in the park.

Sometimes the jokes hurt:

"You only work one hour a week."

"Keep your moving boxes handy; you're probably going to need them soon."

It is hard to live in a fishbowl. It is hard to have every move you make scrutinized and considered. Especially where finances are concerned: "If he can buy a new truck, we are paying him too much." I kid you not. In one place I worked there was a lady who noticed everything. I mean everything. I am serious. If one of the kids wore something new to church, she made a comment about how nice it was to be able to buy new clothes. You can laugh, but I was always afraid to wear new underwear to church. I just knew she would know and make a comment of some kind or another.

Lest you think I am complaining, I am not. Okay, maybe just a little. Remember what we said in the last chapter about mercy and grace? It turns out that both preachers and church members need tons of it from each other. After the murders of Karen and Cole, I needed more mercy and grace than I could ever have imagined. I needed more than most folks around me could have known.

All in all, I have lived a blessed life. I am living a blessed life now. And in case you missed it, I love preaching. Besides, it's a great excuse to write every week! But if you can hear my heart, I'd like to ask two things of you: First, cut your preacher and other church leaders some slack; they need it, just as you do. Second, consider John the Baptist's special calling in life. John knew he had a singular role to fill. He knew because his parents knew. They knew because an angel told them.

Can you imagine? A lot of us have children, and we believe they are the greatest thing since sliced bread. Not to take away from your kids or mine, but John's parents didn't have to dream or imagine or even wonder if greatness was possible. They had the words of the angel Gabriel: "He will be a joy and delight to you, and many will rejoice because of his birth, for he will be great in the sight of the Lord" (Luke 1:14–15).

The Gospels make it clear that John's ministry was a real deal. All four of them give us similar details. Better yet, three of them use almost identically the same words of the prophet Isaiah to describe John's purpose, his mission in life as the forerunner of Jesus.

But John? Even though he is a first cousin to Jesus, it's a wonder we ever heard his message. Talk about a character. Imagine a preacher showing up at your church to talk about Jesus. There is nothing out of the ordinary in that scenario, but imagine a bit more. Think Duck Dynasty showing up. Or maybe even crazy Cousin Eddie from *Christmas Vacation*:

"You surprised to see us, Clark?"

"Oh, Eddie . . . If I woke up tomorrow with my head
sewn to the carpet, I wouldn't be more surprised than I
am now."

In that vein, envision this preacher as poor, unshaved, unwashed,
unkempt, and wearing camouflage hunting clothes that look like
they've have been worn an entire hunting season without ever
meeting the inside of a washing machine. Also, visualize that this
preacher has not an ounce of couth and is not cultured, urbane, or
sophisticated by anyone's standard. He also comes with an overly
developed propensity to tell it as he sees it.

Scripture describes him like this:

John's clothes were made of camel's hair, and he had a
leather belt around his waist. His food was locusts and
wild honey. (Matt. 3:4)

John said to the crowds coming out to be baptized by
him, "You brood of vipers! Who warned you to flee
from the coming wrath? Produce fruit in keeping with
repentance. And do not begin to say to yourselves, 'We
have Abraham as our father.' For I tell you that out of
these stones God can raise up children for Abraham.
The ax is already at the root of the trees, and every tree
that does not produce good fruit will be cut down and
thrown into the fire." (Luke 3:7–9)

A long time ago I owned a camel-hair sport coat. I want one again,
though I don't think what John the Baptist was wearing was quite
so refined. If you add in his language and his let-the-chips-fall-
where-they-may attitude, I doubt he would be welcomed in most
modern church assemblies. We don't like name-calling, and we

certainly want our preachers and messages to be positive, encouraging, and uplifting.

While I am certain John the Baptist was positive, I don't suspect he cared one whit about being encouraging and uplifting. He came with a job description. He came telling truth, calling for personal responsibility, and preaching repentance. He was literally preparing the way for One greater than he—One who would come in the power of the Holy Spirit.

Unfortunately, the world is not always kind to those who speak truth to power. King Herod did not take kindly to being publicly rebuked. John the Baptist was eventually arrested, put in prison, and ultimately beheaded. But before his death, he had time to be fully cognizant of his own humanity. He had time to wonder, fear, question, and doubt. Enough so that even though he had baptized Jesus, witnessed the Spirit of God descending, and heard the voice from heaven declare Jesus the Son of God, his circumstances led him to doubt.

Being the forerunner of Jesus may have sounded exciting, but it certainly wasn't glamorous to be sitting in a first-century Palestinian prison cell. Circumstances are often the culprit in our doubts, and so John asked Jesus through intermediaries, "Are you the one who is to come, or should we expect someone else?" (Matt. 11:3).

I love Jesus's response: "Go back and report to John what you hear and see: The blind receive sight, the lame walk, those who have leprosy are cleansed, the deaf hear, the dead are raised, and the good news is proclaimed to the poor. Blessed is anyone who does not stumble on account of me" (11:4–6).

Like others before me and others to come, my life descended into chaos, and brokenness ruled the day. I couldn't hide it. I couldn't pretend it didn't happen. It was the lead story on the local news. And my circumstances, like John's, gave rise to great confusion, greater questions, and deep, dark doubt.

Are you the One, Jesus? Are you the One?

It took a little while to work through my human anger and pain. It took some time to process and re-evaluate my understanding of God and my role in life. But eventually I came to a greater faith. Eventually I understood with greater clarity, Jesus is the *One!*

With that perspective came a better understanding of Jesus's words just before his conversation with the disciples of John the Baptist: "Whoever does not take up their cross and follow me is not worthy of me. Whoever finds their life will lose it, and whoever loses their life for my sake will find it" (Matt. 10:38–39). While those words were not spoken to John the Baptist, we get to hear them, and this is their simple message: "This life and what happens or doesn't happen is not the ultimate arbitrator of value. Serving Jesus is."

That's what really matters.

That's what really counts.

That's what is most important.

Think about it like this: All your dreams, goals, and ambitions must fit within the greater priority of serving the mission of Jesus. Just as John the Baptist was the forerunner of Jesus, just as he paved or smoothed the way for the Lord's message, we too exist to point others to Jesus. It doesn't matter how cultured we are. It doesn't matter if we wear the latest fashions. It doesn't matter the color of our skin. It doesn't matter our social status or economic situation. It doesn't matter if we are young or old, ugly or beautiful. It only matters that we belong to and serve Jesus.

If you are searching for your purpose or your reason for existence, this is it: we are pavers and smoothers—pointing the world to the One we serve. In that respect, I'd like you to carefully consider all your hurts, hang-ups, afflictions, and adversities. They can be your stumbling stones, or they can be the smooth pavers you use to help someone else. Take your heartache and use it to help others. In the process, you may find your own equilibrium.

May the world see Jesus in our joy.

May they learn of him in our pain.

May they hear with every breath and heartbeat of our lives: Jesus is the *One!*

GOING DEEPER

Read Matthew 3; 11:1–19

1. Would John the Baptist be accepted in your cultural environment today? Why or why not?

2. What was John's purpose? Why was that important?

3. If John were here today, how would you have answered his doubt?

4. What abilities or talents do you have that might be considered God's calling in your life?

5. Do your goals and priorities line up with the goals and priorities of God's Kingdom? Why or why not? What changes do you need to make in order to answer God's call on your life?

Chapter 20

MR. INCREDIBLY IMPULSIVE

But when he saw the wind, he was afraid and, beginning to sink, cried out, "Lord, save me!"

Immediately Jesus reached out his hand and caught him. "You of little faith," he said, "why did you doubt?" —Matthew 14:30–31

A long time ago in a life lived far away, there were a couple of cute, sweet kids at church. They weren't my kids, and unless you are one of two possible people, they weren't your kids either. That narrows it down a good bit, I know. At any rate, one of these kids said to his father when I got up to preach, "Hey, Dad, there's Mr. Incredible."

Not only was he sweet, but smart too. It's nice to be known and recognized, but I digress. The reality is, not many people have ever thought I was incredible. At least, not in a good way. But impulsive? That's a tag that easily, readily, and appropriately comes to mind.

Good old Webster comes in handy at times. In case you've lost your copy, this is how he defines "impulsive" for English-language learners: "Doing things or tending to do things suddenly and without careful thought."

Anybody that knows me knows I have a long history with impulsive. It makes me wonder what Elizabeth Barrett Browning might have written if she was a redneck preacher. Instead of "How do I love thee, let me count the ways," it would have been something along the lines of, "In how many different situations could I be overly impulsive, let me never know the complete answer."

Do you know the famous last words of the dying redneck? "Hey, y'all, watch this!" You can laugh, but my life has been a dictionary, encyclopedia, and picture-book of impulsiveness all rolled into one. Even worse, whenever I had time to think it through or to explore other options, my pride often would not allow me to back down. The result? Impulsiveness ruled—or rued—the day! Let me make this abundantly clear: nothing is more dangerous or stupid than impulsiveness dipped into a vat of pride.

And there it is. Call me Mr. Incredibly Impulsive, the guy with the physical scars, emotional wounds, and spiritual road rash to prove my bona fides. As hard as I try, as much as I'd like to, I cannot restrain my impulsiveness in making this statement: "I am not alone."

I am not all by myself in making bad decisions, poor judgments, and idiotic mistakes. I am not the first guy, nor will I be the last, to leap without looking. Plenty of others have traipsed along with me down the primrose path of opening my mouth before I thought it through.

See yourself yet? The Bible tells us of one person whose proximity to Jesus (as in, he should have known better) makes him the king of impulsive behavior. These days we know him as the apostle Peter. Had he lived in a different time, we might call him the Mouth of the South. Or better yet, the guy most likely to have a bigger impulse drive than anybody else in his Palestinian High graduation class. If the teenage Peter was anything like the adult version, I doubt that his classmates voted him most likely to succeed. Maybe to go to jail or die young, but succeed? Hard to imagine.

Occasionally, as the adage goes, even a blind hog finds an acorn. But, unfortunately for some of us, uncontrolled impulsiveness is not the route normally taken to find success. There are, however, plenty of stories in the New Testament of Peter's impulsiveness, like the one about Peter swinging his sword in John 18. Who can forget how quickly Peter declared Jesus the Messiah and then argued with him in Matthew 16? Did you ever notice how Matthew describes it? "Peter took him aside and began to rebuke him. 'Never, Lord!' he said. 'This shall never happen to you!'" (16:22). Rebuke Jesus? That is about as impulsive as it gets.

These are all good stories that well illustrate Peter's impulsive nature. But my favorite, the one that makes me grin, the one that cements my identity with Peter, is found in Matthew 14:22–33. My imagination goes wild with this story. Try it with me. Imagine being on a small wooden boat.

I see the waves. I feel the wind. My knees flex with the rocking of the boat. I feel the lump of fear that rises in the throat. I experience the visual terror of seeing a ghost. I instinctively get the relief of hearing Jesus's voice. But, more than anything, I know and feel Peter's impulsive words, "Hey, I want to do that!"

Sometimes we read too much into the way Peter frames his question, "Lord, if it's you, tell me to come to you on the water." I think we are too quick to assume doubt on Peter's part, when all he is doing is trying to get his mind wrapped around the scene before him. This isn't a man who is actively questioning Jesus's identity. On the other hand, this is a man living out his natural inclination to impulsiveness.

So, as we see Peter fully in the grip of his impulsive persona, I can feel him sliding across the gunwale. I can see him swing his legs over the side. I watch him drying his hands off on his tunic.

And then there is the little lurch and splash, and his feet slam onto the solid surface of the water.

Solid surface of the water? Yes, that's right. This was not a newfangled way of swimming. This was Mr. Incredibly Impulsive himself standing—that's STANDING, for the hard of hearing—on top of the sea. Not sinking. Not thrashing. Not floundering to stay on top of the water, but standing. And then walking.

Peter was walking on the water just like Jesus. Maybe you can't imagine it, but I see it clearly. I see the huge, wide-eyed look of wonder. I see the possum-eating-grapes grin as it spreads across his face. I see the stutter-dance step of a guy who is milking this moment for all it's worth. I see him make the universal sign (at least in the English-speaking world) of "loser" to his brothers still in the boat.

It's hard to imagine anybody having any more fun out of their impulsiveness. Can you at least reach deep enough to imagine the sheer joy and celebration of such a moment? Surely you have experienced that yourself. Maybe it was graduation or the promotion. Maybe it was hearing her say *yes* and then seeing her walk down the aisle to meet you. Maybe it was the birth of a child. Maybe it was the doctor saying we got it all. Maybe it was the thrill of victory, crossing the finish line, the crack of the bat, the swish of the net, or breaking the plane of the end zone.

From that perspective, don't you just love a good celebration? I suspect Peter did. I suspect he reveled in that moment of connecting with Jesus and experiencing the Creator's mastery of the created. But in a moment so highly reflective of our own lives, the celebration went awry. Like being on the receiving end of a swift uppercut, the joy was staggered as the specter of fear raised its ugly head.

Could this be another experience you have in common with Peter? Maybe he changed his mind about loving you mid-course.

Maybe the baby had problems unseen at first. Maybe the new promotion came with a load too heavy to bear. Maybe the graduation promise fizzled with the economy. Maybe your own body grew old and frail. Maybe the disease came back with a vengeance.

Like Peter, all of us have faced those waves. Like Peter, all of us have been battered by the storm. Like Peter, we have seen doubt creep in not slowly, but descend with force in a moment. Like Peter, all of us have experienced that moment when it seemed that all was lost.

It's not that hard to imagine experiencing the wind and the waves Peter faced. No, if you'll pardon the bad grammar, we got this. We got this in spades. Good old impulsive Peter. Poor old fearful Peter. He is *us* in a nutshell—our lives are encapsulated by the two extremes in this story.

Often when this story is told in a sermon, the focus is first on Peter's amazing faith, and then it shifts to his mistake in taking his eyes off Jesus. I understand the reasoning behind stressing those important details. We do need to understand that faith is enabled and bolstered by keeping our eyes on Jesus. I need to be reminded frequently of how important those concepts are. If you'll further pardon the repetitiveness, I get that, and suspect you do too. But as much as I love this story of Peter's walk on the water, it is Jesus's words and actions I need.

Remember when the disciples first thought Jesus was a ghost? Bible translations differ as to the exact time of early morning it was, but the military has a phrase that perfectly nails it: "zero-dark-thirty." At three or four in the morning, the things you see or hear have a ghostly, fearful quality. Let the phone ring in the middle of the night and your heart will pound and your fears will explode and you will imagine the worse. And sometimes what you imagine comes to fruition. Sometimes what you imagine doesn't come close to the reality. Sometimes it is a train wreck coming, and you are powerless to stop it.

I love Jesus's words to the disciples at that intersection of helplessness and fear: "Take courage! It is I. Don't be afraid" (Matt. 14:27). Then, after the excitement of Peter's water-walking foray turns to fear, Jesus does more than just give audible words. The Bible says, "Immediately Jesus reached out his hand and caught him."

Have you ever stopped to wonder if this story is in the Bible because it is a story we need? I am thankful for the story of impulsive Peter. I am thankful for the example of diving in and trusting the One who is Lord of all and holds all in his hands.

Yes, as hard as it has been to learn this important lesson, I am glad I did.

GOING DEEPER

Read Matthew 8:23–27; 14:22–33

1. How would you describe Peter? What are his best qualities? What are his worst?

2. Was Peter an optimist or a pessimist? How does that outlook affect his life?

3. Describe Peter's faith. What makes Peter an example to follow? What life lessons can you learn from Peter's example?

4. Where do you need to take a risk for God? Is it really a risk if God is involved?

5. What storms has God stilled in your life? What would you say to someone caught up in a fierce storm?

Chapter 21

BENEDICT JUDAS

After he had said this, Jesus was troubled in spirit and testified, "Very truly I tell you, one of you is going to betray me. . . ."

"It is the one to whom I will give this piece of bread when I have dipped it in the dish." Then, dipping the piece of bread, he gave it to Judas, the son of Simon Iscariot. As soon as Judas took the bread, Satan entered into him.

So Jesus told him, "What you are about to do, do quickly."
—John 13:21, 26–27

Have you ever wanted to laugh during a funeral? Seriously? Have you ever had to work hard to suppress a snort in the middle of a church service?

Preachers are the worst at this, from my experience. We are trained, educated, and equipped to be solemn when and where we need to be. But certain verses in certain translations have been known to provoke a struggle to repress the inappropriate laughter of our inner twelve-year-old. Even worse, occasionally someone will read something wrong—out loud in church—and it will be all a guy can do to hold in the laughter.

I will not share any pre-adolescent examples here except for one that is mostly personal with me—and highly indicative of an excessive silliness factor. If this example isn't good enough for you, ask your own preacher for another. Or better yet, read your Bible—you'll find something to make you grin.

I did promise you an example, so here goes. True confession. I cannot read, either privately or publicly, the name "Judas Iscariot" without fighting the inner mental giggle of a third grader. Every time I see his name I want to call him "Judas-is-a-carrot." Beyond silly, I am sure, and there are loads of scholarly opinions on the meaning of "Iscariot." While interesting, they are not what I want to consider.

In US history, numerous traitors have plotted, divided, or otherwise acted in their own self-interests while betraying their country. They are each infamous to some degree, but none so much as Benedict Arnold. In some respects, Benedict was a pitiful character. A capable and worthy commander, he accomplished many good things in the quest for American sovereignty. But disappointment, bitterness, and disillusionment ultimately led to an act of betrayal that has become synonymous with his name.

However, Benedict has nothing on the man Christendom rightly considers the most infamous traitor of all, Judas Iscariot. And since I can't restrain myself, let's just call him Judas.

That's a name that often stirs disgust, disrespect, anger, and almost any other negative emotion found in our English vocabulary. There is nothing much worse than betrayal, and the word Judas says it all. As I already mentioned, I have a grandson named Jude, but you don't hear of many babies being named Judas. Like Hitler, Stalin, or even Osama, Judas evokes little that could be considered pleasant. Some things can be redeemed, but I am not sure Judas or his name ever will be.

Betrayal isn't something we take lightly. American music is full of somebody-done-somebody-wrong songs. Even our lingo and slang are full of ways to describe what betrayal is like.

- Stabbed in the back
- Sold down the river
- Taken for a ride
- Double-crossed
- Spat in my face
- Pulled the wool over my eyes

And in the immortal words of William Shakespeare as he had Julius Caesar speak them, *Et tu Brute?* Even you, Brutus? Even you?

How could you? Those are words we have said to others, or maybe they were said to us. How could you? Nobody likes being thrown under the bus. Nobody likes being the scapegoat. Nobody likes the blame being laid at his or her feet. And nobody, I mean *nobody*, ever enjoys being betrayed, especially by someone we love and trust.

Ask the guy who unknowingly invested his life savings in a Ponzi scheme. Ask the woman who said yes and moved across the country away from family and friends, only to be contemptuously discarded and kicked to the curb for a newer model. Ask the employees who began to build a company, only to learn it was based on deliberately fraudulent information. Have you ever heard the phrase "cooked the books?"

Since we have already invoked the giggle of a third grader, ask the poor kid whose best friend made fun of him on the playground in front of the whole class. How could you? Why would you? Why did you? I think those are questions Jesus could have asked in his humanity. Certainly, considering Judas's betrayal, they are pertinent questions to ask.

As we pick up our story, Jesus is praying in the Garden of Gethsemane. He is already in substantial agony over his coming tribulations, and his most intimate disciples are not very supportive. Into this mix of swirling emotions comes one of Jesus's inner circle with poisoned heart and envenomed lips. With a kiss, Judas's betrayal was done.

All these centuries later, nothing about Judas's reputation has truly been rehabilitated. There is no commission to overthrow the guilty verdict. There is no organization intent on seeing him in a fairer light. I would like to be remembered, but not like this. No, Judas will go down in history as the worst betrayer of all time. That he did it with the intimacy of a kiss only elevates it to a higher level of disgust. If you are like me, you probably can't even begin to say something as simple as "poor old Judas."

Unfortunately, long before this ugly affair, there were problems in Judas's character, and those problems created even more problems, leading to his ultimate betrayal. John 12 tells the story of Mary, sister to Lazarus and Martha, anointing Jesus's feet with a pint of pure nard, "an expensive perfume" (12:3). We then learn of Judas's strident objection and the true reason behind it: "Why wasn't this perfume sold and the money given to the poor? It was worth a year's wages." He said this, John tells us, "not because he cared about the poor but because he was a thief; as keeper of the money bag, he used to help himself to what was put into it" (12:5–6).

During Jesus's earthly ministry, a ministry Judas was fully immersed in, Jesus taught his disciples many wonderfully important, life-affirming lessons. Maybe you'll remember these two from the Sermon on the Mount that Judas either conveniently forgot or never understood in the first place:

> Do not store up for yourselves treasures on earth, where moths and vermin destroy, and where thieves break in and steal. But store up for yourselves treasures in heaven, where moths and vermin do not destroy, and where thieves do not break in and steal. For where your treasure is, there your heart will be also. (Matt. 6:19–21)

No one can serve two masters. Either you will hate the
one and love the other, or you will be devoted to the one
and despise the other. You cannot serve both God and
money. (Matt. 6:24)

Do you see where Judas's heart was? Do you see the internal and
external conflict he was living in? I have been a Judas neophyte
most of my preaching life. I can't remember ever preaching a
sermon on Judas. I can't remember ever doing much thinking
about him at all. Most of my theology where Judas is concerned
could be summed up and communicated quite clearly in six short
words or two short phrases: "Judas bad. Don't be like Judas."

Suffice it to say I was quite surprised to learn that there are several other theories or possibilities for why Judas did what he did.
I would have assumed that Judas's betrayal was primarily moti-
vated by greed, especially given what we learned of him in John 12.
However, some believe Judas's actions were intended to force Jesus
to confront the power of Rome. Others believe that Judas betrayed
out of disillusionment, out of his own sense of being betrayed by
Jesus's proclamations of impending death.

So, which was it? Was it greed? Was it confrontation? Was it
disillusionment? Yes, it was. I have no problem saying yes to any
of those statements, yes to them individually or yes to them as one
combined answer. Yes. And it ought to scare us to death.

If the answer is greed, that should scare us, because I don't
know anybody who hasn't struggled with materialism. I don't
know anybody who isn't tempted to allow the things of this world
to become our treasure, to be what we serve.

As far as confrontation is concerned, many of us have bar-
gained with God, trying to get him to work within our own agenda.
And disillusionment? Who hasn't been disappointed by God?
Who hasn't been tempted to take matters into our hands when

God doesn't do what we expect or want? (Remember the warning about vengeance belonging to God? That's an inconvenient verse for many of us.)

Nobody wants to be compared to Judas, but there it is. Like Judas, every single one of us is susceptible to betraying God. John 13:27 tells us that after Judas ate the bread, Satan entered him. Bryant and Krause note that "ironically for Judas, the bread of the Last Supper was not 'Christ's body broken for him,' but his commitment to self-serving allegiance and evil actions."[1] In Judas's desire for whatever was not of God, he became the tool of Satan.

In my faith tradition, we partake of the Lord's Supper every Sunday. It is a hallowed, holy moment of reflection, communion, and remembrance. I just wonder how many times we eat of the bread and drink of the cup and then turn right around and betray our Lord. Suddenly, I don't feel quite so superior to Judas.

In your struggles for the legal tender, in your wanting God to do a certain thing, in your disappointment when God doesn't do what you think God should have done, guard your heart. Don't become a tool for Satan. The reality of Judas isn't very far from any of us.

GOING DEEPER

Read John 13:1–30; Mark 14:43–50

1. Think of a time from your childhood when you made something silly that was supposed to be serious. How did the adults react and why?

2. Have you ever been betrayed? What were the consequences? Did you find it easy or hard to forgive?

3. Have you ever betrayed someone? What were the consequences? Did you find it easy or hard to find forgiveness?

4. How did Judas get off track? How did you?

5. What betrayals of Jesus do you struggle with now?

6. Who do you need to ask for mercy and grace? To whom do you need to give mercy and grace?

Note

[1]Beauford H. Bryant and Mark S. Krause, *The College Press NIV Commentary on John* (Joplin, MO: College Press, 1998), 292.

Chapter 22

MR. JEW

On that day a great persecution broke out against the church in Jerusalem, and all except the apostles were scattered throughout Judea and Samaria. Godly men buried Stephen and mourned deeply for him. But Saul began to destroy the church. Going from house to house, he dragged off both men and women and put them in prison. —Acts 8:1–3

I have no memories of extreme financial difficulty as a young child. I know that after my third-grade year, my dad went back to school to prepare for ministry. Like most people in that kind of situation, it wasn't always easy for my parents. After Dad completed that phase of his education and began working with a church, we weren't extremely well off by American standards. We adjusted. Mom worked to help make ends meet. Looking back, I can see how they tried to live frugally. I know where they tried to save pennies while stretching their dollars.

It was long after I was grown with teenage children of my own before I realized how much it helped my parents for me to start working when I was thirteen. I worked as a shoeshine boy, ran a paper route, and helped at a little country store. Having a job all through my teenage years meant buying my own clothes and anything else I wanted. This made possible two very significant things, one of which was far more important to me at the time: Mom and

Dad could do other things with their money, and (I cannot over-stress the vital, life-affirming importance of this) I didn't have to wear Sears Tough Skins or JCPenny Plain Pocket Jeans.

If you never wore those items, you cannot imagine how significant this change was. It's a wonder I'm not in therapy for those few short years when I had to wear them. (Mom, if you are reading this, I blame Dad solely.)

The truth is, we weren't poor, but we made the economics of our little corner of the world work as best we could. We had the best education money couldn't buy (for those who don't know, that's public schooling). We rode the bus until we could pay for our own gas. Dad didn't give us boys money to take a girl out on a date. If we wanted something, we figured out how to earn and save the money to get it. We were never in any danger of living beyond our means. Nobody could ever say the Ferguson kids were a part of any elite circles. Our lives were modest but full of family love.

From that perspective, I don't readily identify with the man who became the apostle Paul. It's hard for me to find common ground with a guy who so easily could become radicalized. I have thought of that a lot in our age of terrorism. It seems that every time you turn around, somebody from what we would view as a normal walk of life, with a normal background and peaceful family, turns into a fanatic intent on murder and mayhem. Not too long ago, somebody who attended school with two of our boys was arrested at college for involvement in a terrorist plot.

How does that happen? How does that happen in Mississippi? What are the factors? How does upbringing, religion, and socio-economics play into radicalization—especially self-radicalization? Nobody bought or read this book thinking they finally were going to get all the information and interpretation leading to the perfect, one-size-fits-all answer. But just in case you wanted to know, I am going to bless you with my short, sweet theory.

Radicalization occurs when someone has been hurt in some fashion by a system they blame. Or, radicalization occurs when someone is more highly educated, frustrated, and certain he knows better than others.

Want a prime example of that second theory? Meet Saul, whom we also call Paul.

In Paul's own words, he was an elite kind of guy. He had the pedigree, the education, the connections. He had all the right stuff. Consider how he said it on the steps of the Temple in Jerusalem: "I am a Jew, born in Tarsus of Cilicia, but brought up in this city. I studied under Gamaliel and was thoroughly trained in the law of our ancestors" (Acts 22:3).

The school of Gamaliel wasn't a boarding school for wayward youth. This was the crème of the crème. Paul was trained as rabbi, lawyer, and teacher. He was a citizen of Rome with all privileges pertaining to, wherewith, hitherto, and thereof. He was, by his upbringing, training, and faith, a Jew of Jews. See how he describes himself: "Circumcised on the eighth day, of the people of Israel, of the tribe of Benjamin, a Hebrew of Hebrews; in regard to the law, a Pharisee" (Phil. 3:5).

Like I said, Paul was in many respects an elite kind of guy. He wore Brooks Brothers suits, Armani shoes, carried around a handmade Italian leather briefcase (hey, he was headed to Rome anyway), argued cases before the Supremes, and was chauffeured everywhere he went.

Not really, but you get the picture. Paul was a big dog who didn't have to stay on the porch. Paul was the *man*. Paul knew who he was and where he was going, and the only direction was up.

In Paul's mind, there was something distasteful about those pesky followers of the Nazarene. They and their weird claims offended him. They were an affront to his sense of propriety. They didn't stand much for decorum. They were common folk—the kind who caught his dinner, made his furniture, and otherwise took care of the things he needed to be comfortable. Worse, they wouldn't shut-up about the crucified Jesus—a loser pretending to be something he wasn't. They upset his equilibrium.

I don't know how damaged Paul was by their claims—there may have been some hurt in the presumed rejection of what he believed in. After all, it's not every day a ragamuffin, ruffian group comes along and says you have it all wrong. As Sweet Brown explained on the news and later to the world on YouTube, "Ain't nobody got time for that!"

It takes no leap of faith for me to believe that Saul who would be Paul felt both frustrated and obligated to help these benighted people—or rather, force them—to see the fallacy of their belief. And when they refused? Paul said he was fanatical in his pursuit:

> "I was just as zealous for God as any of you are today.
> I persecuted the followers of this Way to their death,
> arresting both men and women and throwing them
> into prison, as the high priest and all the Council can
> themselves testify. I even obtained letters from them to
> their associates in Damascus, and went there to bring
> these people as prisoners to Jerusalem to be punished."
> (Acts 22:3–5)

To give you a greater perspective, Paul said his zeal was based on persecuting the church—and he did so with a righteousness based on the Law (Phil. 3:6). There is every reason to believe the radicalized Saul/Paul was a true believer in what he said and did. Apparently, he was good at it, too.

Poor old Saul/Paul. Even with all his upbringing, training, education, experience, and zeal, he was no match for the crucified and risen Jesus. And since we are using the metaphor of wrestling, maybe you can imagine that Saul/Paul got hung up on the turnbuckles and pinned to the mat when he met Jesus on the Damascus Road. If you remember the story, by the time the conversation between Jesus and Paul was over, he had to be led by the hand into the city. Acts 9:9 goes on to tell us, "For three days he was blind, and did not eat or drink anything."

Can you imagine the blow this must have been to his pride and ego? Live long enough and you too will have one of those shocking, life-changing moments where all the answers you thought you had turn out to be worthless. I have had to eat my share of crow over the years. I have been wrong and proven wrong. It is almost always a humbling experience. On occasion, it has been absolutely humiliating.

In the flashing light of heaven, the Jesus Paul had ridiculed, laughed at, and despised became the ultimate reality of life, the crucified and risen Lord. In the flashing light of heaven, Paul came face to face with the foolishness of the Cross and the weakness of God, and it changed everything. Continuing in his story, Paul was baptized and began a new life, a new journey of following the One he had devoted his life to persecuting. It was the beginning of his whole world being turned upside down. It certainly wasn't what Paul envisioned when he began his journey to Damascus.

If you are at all like me, then you are somewhat like Paul. Maybe you are not as well off or well-educated. Maybe you don't have the kind of connections he had. Maybe you don't see your own self-worth the way Paul obviously saw his. But like Paul we are. When we know what we are talking about, we have all the answers. When we don't know what we are talking about? Well, that doesn't stop most of us from pretending that we have all the answers.

Let me be blunt and write from my own foibles. Some of you have all the theological answers. You have the academics, knowledge, training, and expertise to back it up. Some of you have all the political answers. Just a quick glimpse at your Facebook account assures us that you are a fount of knowledge, opinion, and wisdom gained over years of talking around the water cooler.

Some of you have all the relational answers. You have been around the block a time or two and have it all figured out. Give you the slightest opening and you can fix any problem, large or small. Or maybe it's parenting, or losing weight, or how to do new math. All we must do is listen to you. It'll all be okay—take two aspirin and call me in the morning. The funny thing is, after you have dispensed your wisdom and assured us that you are not the least bit smug, arrogant, or condescending, you remain frustrated when we don't do exactly what your wisdom calls for.

I get it, because I am just like you. Wiser. Smarter. More intelligent. Experienced. Gifted. Knowledgeable. Just listen to me and save yourself some trouble. Seriously. If you are reading with one eye closed, now is the time to sit up and pay attention. Now is the time to really listen: any answer that doesn't begin and end with Jesus isn't an answer at all!

In the flashing, blinding light of heaven, Paul learned that nothing else in his life mattered. Paul discovered that his education didn't count. Paul learned how little value was found in his pedigree. Paul painfully discovered that his zeal was misplaced. On the road to Damascus, Paul learned what we must discover: it's all Jesus, all the time. When you understand that, it changes everything!

GOING DEEPER

Read Acts 7:51–8:3; 9:1–19

1. Saul/Paul's zealousness or fanaticism took him into dangerous territory. What did he seemingly justify or feel good about?

2. After his conversion, Saul/Paul was still fanatical. How was his fanaticism different?

3. How does fanaticism shape us or warp us? Are there things worthy of our fanaticism?

4. What are you fanatical about?

5. If the converted Saul/Paul was your example, what would change or be different in your life?

Chapter 23

THE INVITATION MAN

The Word became flesh and made his dwelling among us. We have seen his glory, the glory of the one and only Son, who came from the Father, full of grace and truth. —John 1:14

I cannot remember a time when church wasn't the backdrop of my life. In fact, most of my earliest memories revolve around church. Apart from two separate six-month foreign deployments at sea while in the U.S. Navy, I cannot recall any period where I missed two weeks or more in church. I tell you this not to pat myself on the back or to set myself up as a standard. To the contrary, I am illustrating to you how much influence the church has had in my life. With few exceptions, my friends, family, and social connections have primarily come through being an active part of a church family—even when I wasn't a minister.

I love the church. She has disappointed me at times. Even shattered me on occasion. But I believe with all my heart that she is the Bride of Christ and is due my love and affection. But honestly? As much as I love church, sometimes I get weary of church folks. I am trying to say that nicely. This isn't a mean-spirited thing at all. Like I said, sometimes I get tired of church folks.

Sometimes it is me. It could be a struggle with some issue or difficulty in my life. Sometimes my heart hits an obstinate patch.

Sometimes I am just exhausted and overwhelmed with all the activity and busyness. Let's be real; we can be busier than a whole den of busy beavers carrying sticks from one place to another. We don't always do a good job of seeking rest.

But if I am going to be completely honest with nothing held back, sometimes it is you. Sometimes I just cannot live up to the high standards that are forced upon me by people who are not meeting those same standards themselves. Sometimes it is your condescension or judgmental attitudes and actions. Sometimes it is your holier-than-thou-better-than-everybody-else routine. Frankly, I don't do well with criticism and second-guessing. I'm not alone in that regard either.

What's worse? Sometimes I do the same things to you. I don't know if it violates a ministry clause somewhere, but there are days when I have a love/hate relationship with people I am supposed to be in fellowship with. There are days when I feel compelled to grin and take it, smile and fake it. There are days when I join the vast crowds at church in the time-honored tradition of looking you in the eyes and lying through my teeth. Yes, like you, I participate in telling the greatest lie ever told in church—on Sundays, no less.

"I'm fine. Everything is great. We are all good. Everything is fine. I am fine."

We tell that lie, and outwardly we don't even flinch. In fact, though we may have initially died a little bit inside when we first felt the need to pretend that life was perfect and all was good, we quickly grew proficient and comfortable with those help-inhibiting words.

I'm fine. I tell you that because I cannot handle your disapproving stares. I tell you that because you can't handle me where I am. I tell you that because to do otherwise would disrupt your little fantasy world where everybody and everything is copasetic. Yes, we like to cling to the fantasy of a happy-go-lucky existence where everything is peaches and cream. I wonder how many times God looks down on us and says to himself, "No, no, no, that's not how I want you to be together in my family!" I wonder if it's like looking through smoke.

That's how I often see Jesus when I try to see him through you. He's blurry and none-too-clear. I am positive that there are times when you see Jesus in me much the same way. When I am condescending, arrogant, or loftier, Jesus is masked, if not outright hidden, in me. When you are judgmental, critical, and superior, Jesus is masked, if not outright hidden, in you.

Come on, church! We can do better than that. We are better than that.

Every character I have written about in this book thus far has been broken, flawed, and imperfect. Every. Single. One. Of. Them. Even the folks we call heroes of the faith were fellow-strugglers on the road of life. None of them had it all together all the time. Every single one of them was found to be needy, broken, God-dependent followers.

My approach has been to look at them sideways. To see beyond the flat page. To consider multiple dimensions. To put ourselves in their shoes. To wonder what they struggled with. To question the possibility of doubt. To try and feel their fear or pain. To marvel at their direction despite ill-fitting comfort zones and personalities that clashed with their directives. To see them face their fears and go with God regardless.

We have talked about Old Testament characters. We have looked at New Testament personalities. There are plenty more we can consider. And with apologies to those included or not, none is worthy of our attention more than Jesus, the Son of God. He wasn't broken, but he was. For all of humanity. For every single, broken, messed-up, stubborn, selfish one of us.

Remember the words of Martha? "Yes, Lord," she replied, "I believe that you are the Messiah, the Son of God, who is to come into the world" (John 11:27). Or how about Peter's confession: "You are the Messiah, the Son of the living God" (Matt. 16:16)? What do those confessions mean? Better yet, what do you do with declarations like that? Theology provides lots of good, right, and needed answers to those questions. But I am not looking to see what kind of theological chops you have. I am not trying to grasp the depth of your understanding and knowledge of doctrine. This isn't about what Scriptures you can quote or shower me with. This is about Jesus. Jesus is my doctrine. Everything flows from him. If you know doctrine but don't know Jesus, your doctrine will leave you cold and miserable.

Who is Jesus? I call him the Invitation Man. I am sure you'll see the connection in the story of the disciple we typically refer to as "Doubting Thomas." You remember him, right? Even as one of the Twelve, Thomas is not all that remarkable. In fact, he is only mentioned once each in the Gospels of Matthew, Mark, and Luke.

But this story is different. Thomas is front and center. If you were following along in John 20, Thomas is having a hard time believing that Jesus has risen from the dead. Famously, he told his fellow disciples, "Unless I see the nail marks in his hands and put my finger where the nails were, and put my hand into his side, I will not believe" (20:25).

You know the old saw about famous last words coming back to bite you? A week later, Thomas is with the disciples again and Jesus appears. He has a singular message for Thomas, "Put your finger here; see my hands. Reach out your hand and put it into my side. Stop doubting and believe" (20:27). I can almost hear and see how Thomas responds. Not the words, for we know exactly what he said. No, I can easily imagine his pale, sallow complexion and hear his bare, throaty whisper, "My Lord and my God!" (20:28).

I love this story. I particularly love the part that tells us Thomas was from Missouri. You may not see that in the text, but you can count on the simple fact that he was from the Show-Me State. I don't know about you (okay, that's a little bit of a fudge, I am quite sure I do), but this is where I have spent almost my entire life.

If you tell me you love me, I am not going to believe it until you show me. If you tell me I am your friend, I am not going to count on it until you show me. Jesus understood that's where Thomas was. Jesus understood that's where we may be. So he extends the most amazing invitation to us through the man we disparagingly call Doubting Thomas: "Put your finger here; see my hands. Reach out your hand and put it into my side. Stop doubting and believe" (20:27).

That's the invitation of Jesus that echoes and resounds still today. We are invited!

Jesus says: See me. Touch me. Know me.

This is not the invitation to know the caricature of Jesus in modern religion—a hunk with flowing locks, chiseled features, and romance-novel allure. This is not an invitation to just know Jesus as a miracle worker walking on water and providing endless fish and chips. After all, Jesus himself said, "Very truly I tell you, you are looking for me, not because you saw the signs I performed but because you ate the loaves and had your fill" (John 6:26).

As true, evocative, and life-changing as the stories about Jesus are, this is an invitation to know far more than chronologies and facts. This is an open invitation to look deep into Jesus's words, life, and identity. This is an ongoing invitation to gaze into the heart of a King. This is an invitation to join him in his Reign. This is an invitation to intimacy.

How have we missed this? How have we taken the stories of Jesus and reduced them to a series of legends to be picked apart and questioned? How have we allowed his life, ministry, and sacrifice to become ho-hum? How have we allowed Jesus to be worthy of academic study and yet somehow not quite the scalpel that flays us open?

I am tired of the superficial Jesus. I am sure you know him. He's the one that gets invoked on Sunday. He's the one we claim to follow who makes no appreciable difference in our heart, attitudes, words, and actions. I am tired of that Jesus. He's not real.

Listen to how Paul said it:

> So it was with me, brothers and sisters. When I came to you, I did not come with eloquence or human wisdom as I proclaimed to you the testimony about God. For I resolved to know nothing while I was with you except Jesus Christ and him crucified. I came to you in weakness with great fear and trembling. My message and my preaching were not with wise and persuasive words, but with a demonstration of the Spirit's power, so that your faith might not rest on human wisdom, but on God's power. (1 Cor. 2:1–5)

That's the Jesus I want to know. The Jesus who leaves you weak and trembling. The Jesus who unequivocally declares that love and service to others—even death on a cross—is what matters. It's not our arguments. It's not our differences of opinion. It's not our posturing. None of that matters. It's Jesus. Only Jesus. All Jesus. He is our doctrine. Everything flows from him. He is the invitation!

Do you know him?

In the words of Philip to Nathaniel, "Come and see" (John 1:46).

GOING DEEPER

Read Genesis 1:1; John 1:1–18, 20:19–29

1. Why is it important to understand Jesus's identity as God?

2. What does it mean to confess Jesus? How does that confession play out in your life?

3. Sometimes our church experience or even our church life is superficial. Is that a product of not truly grasping Jesus's identity? What would change in our churches if we confessed Jesus as he truly is?

4. What role does doubt play in your life? How do you reconcile doubt and faith?

5. What is Jesus inviting you to?

Chapter 24

THE HEART OF THE MAN

They went to Capernaum, and when the Sabbath came, Jesus went into the synagogue and began to teach. The people were amazed at his teaching, because he taught them as one who had authority, not as the teachers of the law. Just then a man in their synagogue who was possessed by an impure spirit cried out, "What do you want with us, Jesus of Nazareth? Have you come to destroy us? I know who you are—the Holy One of God!"

"Be quiet!" said Jesus sternly. "Come out of him!" The impure spirit shook the man violently and came out of him with a shriek.

The people were all so amazed that they asked each other, "What is this? A new teaching—and with authority! He even gives orders to impure spirits and they obey him." News about him spread quickly over the whole region of Galilee. —Mark 1:21-28

To Tell the Truth was an old, 1960s-era game show. Each episode featured three people who all claimed to be the same person. The object was for the celebrity panel to figure who the real person was and who were the imposters. After the panel members had made their selections, the question was finally asked, "Will the real _____ please stand up?"

Sometimes I wonder if that is a legitimate way to find out who is the real Jesus. Will the real Jesus please stand up? Who is Jesus?

Years ago, I used some Bible class and preaching curriculum that had our entire church family studying Jesus for a whole year. The material was deep and compelling. Nothing about it was shallow. In fact, to adequately cover and understand all of it was a huge challenge. Even those of us who thought we knew all the stories had our eyes opened to a Jesus we had never considered before.

We saw him in the Old Testament; we viewed him in the New. We explored his birth narrative and wept over his dying. We rejoiced over his resurrection and were amazed at his ascension. In the Gospels, we marveled at his miracles while wrestling with his teaching. We sat spellbound at his engagement with sinners, and we saw ourselves. We couldn't miss that. We couldn't miss that no matter how hard we tried.

Yes, we saw our failures and flaws through the eyes of Jesus. We were mesmerized by the depth of his mercy. We were shocked by the extent of his love. Together, we grappled with the story of Jesus. We wouldn't be the first nor the last church family to wrestle with his reality. It's what you do when confronted with such amazing grace.

In reading these words, most likely nothing I have said so far leads you to believe anything new or different about Jesus. That's because none of this is new or earth-shattering. We are not breaking innovative ground where academics and scholarship are concerned. There will not be a future Wikipedia article stating that Les Ferguson Jr. is widely recognized for sharing cutting-edge information on Jesus. Not by a long shot. Not this guy. The fact is, you know this stuff. You probably were raised on it. There is nothing novel about Jesus unless you are stunned by a God who would die for you. There will be no surprises, unless you are surprised by forgetting.

Who is Jesus? We know what Peter claimed. We know what Martha said. We know the stories, and I am thankful for that.

Unfortunately, we have fallen prey over the centuries to recreating Jesus in our image.

White America has its own art representations. Black America has exclusive pictures and paintings reflecting a particular cultural milieu. Even Nazi Germany, as reprehensible as it was, had its own Aryan images of Jesus. Before you get on your high horse about how revolting the Nazis were for reimagining Jesus in their sick manner, be quick to remember, we do the same thing.

Dare I mention the political Jesus? Depending on your perspective, Jesus is a Democrat or a Republican. Jesus is a Libertarian or a Socialist. For that matter, we might as well acknowledge the Jesus who would be an Independent.

I hope you are uncomfortable. We spend too much time on a Jesus that doesn't exist except in our minds, hearts, desires, and agendas. Worse, we sometimes forget that Isaiah 53 tells us there was nothing special about the appearance of Jesus.

When Samuel was trying to discern which sons of Jesse would be anointed king, God reminded him of something we need to remember: "Do not consider his appearance or his height, for I have rejected him. The LORD does not look at the things people look at. People look at the outward appearance, but the LORD looks at the heart" (1 Sam. 16:7). We so easily get focused on appearance. We rarely go deep. We often fail to see the heart and what makes it beat.

Do we do the same thing where Jesus is concerned? Do we miss those things we really need to remember? I am sure we do, but in our rush to know the humanity of Jesus, we must not forget his divinity too:

> The Son is the image of the invisible God, the firstborn
> over all creation. For in him all things were created:
> things in heaven and on earth, visible and invisible,

whether thrones or powers or rulers or authorities; all
things have been created through him and for him. He
is before all things, and in him all things hold together.
(Col. 1:15–17)

Isn't that astounding? Jesus is the raw, untamed power that created this amazingly complex world. Jesus is the refined harnessed
power that keeps it all in motion. We shouldn't be all that surprised when Jesus exerts his will and power over creation. He
created the winds and the waves. He can stop them, and he did.
He defied the laws of nature because he wrote them. It was always
his prerogative. He healed the sick and raised the dead because all
things are under his feet. Who's going to stop him?

So how about this: Jesus is Jesus, the Messiah, Savior, and Lord.
Son of God. Prince of Peace. King of Kings. Lord of Glory. The
Lion of the Tribe of Judah! I want you to get that. I need you to
see him. I want you to be awed. I need you to recognize his glory.
I want you to be amazed. I need you to know Jesus. I want you to
be humbled in the presence of The Great I Am!

Why? Because a day will come—if it is not here already—
when you are going to know how great your need is. It may happen
over time. It may come in a powerful, bone-jarring, life-crushing
instant. And when you recognize your need, another beautiful,
life-affirming aspect of Jesus changes everything.

Consider this familiar story:

Jesus returned to Galilee in the power of the Spirit, and
news about him spread through the whole countryside.
He was teaching in their synagogues, and everyone
praised him.

He went to Nazareth, where he had been brought
up, and on the Sabbath day he went into the synagogue,
as was his custom. He stood up to read, and the scroll of

the prophet Isaiah was handed to him. Unrolling it, he found the place where it is written:

> "The Spirit of the Lord is on me,
>   because he has anointed me
>   to proclaim good news to the poor.
> He has sent me to proclaim freedom for the prisoners
>   and recovery of sight for the blind,
> to set the oppressed free,
>   to proclaim the year of the Lord's favor."

Then he rolled up the scroll, gave it back to the attendant and sat down. The eyes of everyone in the synagogue were fastened on him. He began by saying to them, "Today this scripture is fulfilled in your hearing." (Luke 4:14–21)

This, in a nutshell, is the purpose of Jesus. This is the heart of the man we call Savior and Friend. Jesus is good news. Jesus is freedom. Jesus is sight. Jesus is the end of oppression. Jesus himself said, "The thief comes only to steal and kill and destroy; I have come that they may have life, and have it to the full" (John 10:10).

The abundant life isn't what you think. Forget prosperity and materialism. This isn't about your career success or the house of your dreams. This isn't about owning the latest or claiming your status. Jesus's brother understood: "Now listen, you who say, 'Today or tomorrow we will go to this or that city, spend a year there, carry on business and make money.' Why, you do not even know what will happen tomorrow. What is your life? You are a mist that appears for a little while and then vanishes" (James 4:13–14).

Life is so much more than the here and now. In fact, you may very well have oppression in this world. You may know blindness in this life. You may struggle with pain and heartache. You may have occasion to ask a thousand times, why? why? why?

I hope you'll get real in a way what I missed for too many years of my life: Jesus never said, "Follow me and you will live a life without difficulty." Jesus never promised an existence here that was painless and free. We would do well to remember that Jesus said the exact opposite: "I have told you these things, so that in me you may have peace. In this world, you will have trouble. But take heart! I have overcome the world" (John 16:33).

So here's to real good news. Here's to real freedom. Here's to the end of oppression. Here's to true vision. Here's to a better life. Here's to an abundant life in Jesus—a life that never ends.

It's not always easy to remember that. The abundant life isn't always clearly understood, especially as we live in what Paul calls "jars of clay" (2 Cor. 4:7). I don't know about you, but my body is far from perfect. Whoever said "Growing old is not for sissies" nailed it. In fact, there is much in your life and mine that serves as visual reminders of what Paul said about being hard-pressed, perplexed, persecuted, and struck down. Most of us know from personal experience that life can be incredibly painful. But Paul also tells us in those same verses that each of those situations is not the final condition. There is always more to the story. And so he goes on to say, "We know that the one who raised the Lord Jesus from the dead will also raise us with Jesus" (2 Cor. 4:14).

Whatever has happened in your life, whatever may be happening now, or what you may know to be still coming down the pike, it's not the final story. The power that raised Jesus from the dead can and will give new life, new meaning, to your story. If not now, then.

See the heart of Jesus.

Fix your eyes on him.

His resurrection means yours too!

GOING DEEPER

Read Mark 1:21–45; 2 Corinthians 4:7–8; Colossians 1:15–20

1. How is Jesus's authority acknowledged or recognized in your life?

2. In what area of your life do you find yourself rejecting his authority?

3. What attribute of Jesus gives you the most peace, joy, hope?

4. What makes your life abundant?

5. What aspect of Jesus do you need to wrestle with most? Why?

Chapter 25

THE WEAKNESS OF GOD, PART ONE

So Jacob was left alone, and a man wrestled with him till daybreak.
When the man saw that he could not overpower him, he touched the
socket of Jacob's hip so that his hip was wrenched as he wrestled with
the man. Then the man said, "Let me go, for it is daybreak."
But Jacob replied, "I will not let you go unless you bless me."
—Genesis 32:24–26

I used this same passage back in Chapter Eight. I need you to consider it again, this time in a different light. I have never been much of a wrestler—at least the kind who uses special moves and holds. At my age, I still don't want my father to put me in a head-lock. While I was never really all that strong, I never knew how weak I could be.

I have struggled most of my adult life with being overweight and out of shape. Several times over the years, I achieved the weight loss I desired, but it never lasted very long. At least three times in my life, I got on a running kick that gave me some results, though never as quickly or as long-lasting as I would have liked. Two or three times, I delved somewhat passionately into strength and weight training. Occasionally I got to the place where I could see a bicep, but just barely.

Back in Chapter Thirteen, I mentioned starting a training regimen, a four-day-a-week fitness boot camp. What was I thinking? Having been through boot camp in the U.S. Navy, I should have been smarter than that.

Running, jumping, crawling, planks, weights, burpees, and other weird, hard stuff became my daily routine. As painful as it was, I discovered amazing things about myself. But first, I discovered just how weak I could be.

Push-ups? I could barely do one.

Planks? Who am I kidding?

Sit-ups? This is a joke, right?

It was pitiful. I was pitiful. I was certifiably weak, physically and mentally. Mr. T would look at me and say, "I pity the fool." And I hurt. Oh, how I hurt!! How bad did I hurt? I took baths. I soaked in Epsom salt. I popped ibuprofen tablets as if they were breath mints for a bad case of halitosis. I bought braces—multiple kinds. I slathered on Icy Hot and Biofreeze. I watched TV at night with ice packs on my knees. Again, Mr. T would look at me and say, "I pity the fool."

Physical weakness is one thing, but spiritual weakness is another whole story. As it turns out, again, I never knew how weak I could be. At least, not back then in the old life I once lived.

There I was. Like any other person of faith, I had my difficulties and challenges. Sometimes those struggles led to questions that weren't all that easy to resolve. Sometimes those challenges were people. But I was the preacher. I was the minister. Not only was I on staff, I also served as one of our elders. I was shepherd in both name and deed.

I could not allow myself to dwell on my struggles and questions. I couldn't invest the time and energy in me that I needed. Or rather, I didn't. That's where my other fears and flaws grew bigger. Fears of failure. Fears of irrelevance. Fears of not having the right answers. Fears of not knowing how to satisfy challenging people. Ultimately those unanswered questions, those unresolved fears were like an old-fashioned pressure cooker. Sooner or later it was going to pop. And when tragedy reared its ugly head, pop it did.

Still, I never thought my faith could be so easily shaken. Shaken may be an understatement. Shattered may be closer to the truth. When life unraveled, I was shocked at how far and how quickly I could fall. I was shocked because I believed.

I believed. My entire life was based and had been based around my belief. Let me remind you: I have never quit believing in God. Never once have I doubted his existence. I believed. I believed then; I believe now. But as I have said before, I got to a place where I doubted God's love, care, and concern for me. I doubted whether God had my best interests at heart. I doubted whether I mattered at all. Hard stuff for a guy at any age.

Wrestling with God is exhausting. But I had been there before. I had wrestled with God in my past. One of my earliest memories involves wrestling with God. I distinctly recall asking my mother with some trepidation and even indignation about the fate of the animals at the end of time. I was in first or second grade. I could not reconcile my image of God with the destruction of the world.

Can you imagine a kid that young wrestling with God? Seriously, can you? You should. It happens all the time. It happens here in our land. It happens in far-flung places. It happens next door. And whether you want to acknowledge it or not, it happens right there in your church family. It might be happening even now in your own home.

Really? Yes, really. Wrestling with God happens all the time. It happens in classrooms, breakrooms, and jail visitation rooms.

It happens in doctor's offices, hospital rooms, and boardrooms. It happens in funeral homes and cemeteries.

Whatever starts the wrestling match doesn't have to be earth-shattering or macabre. It could begin in Sunday school or worship. It might start during private study. It sometimes happens in group discussions. Without reservation, it happens in the still, quiet moments of the night where doubts arise and fears materialize unbidden.

Wrestling with God is not a bad thing. In fact, if the story of Jacob is any indication, God likes to wrestle with us. Wrestling is a growth opportunity. Wrestling is a time of stretching. Wrestling is recognition of One who is greater than I.

I love the way God wrestles. This isn't a sumo match with a fat guy crushing the life out of you. This isn't professional TV wrestling with a muscle-bound dude bashing your head in with a metal folding chair. Did I mention the weakness of God? That's how he wrestles.

Back in Genesis 3, Satan decided to wrestle with God in a series of matches. He had some pretty slick moves. The first match finds Satan throwing down Adam and Eve. It was a preliminary grudge match leading to the main event between God and Satan.

As the story continues, Adam and Eve, who had formerly enjoyed time with God in the Garden, were now actively hiding from him. We know from the creation account that they were unashamed of their nakedness, but with Satan's deceit and their defeat, the gig is up.

Adam and Eve's loss was immediate and total. They were demolished. While Satan celebrated, he was completely unaware of the shellacking he was taking. He thought he was relishing his initial victory, unaware that his hat had been handed to him in a vicious defeat. Even as God pronounced his curse on Satan and promised his ultimate destruction, I am not sure Satan understood. God was playing a long game that Satan couldn't quite see.

And that brings us back to us. The echoes of Adam and Eve's defeat are like ripples in time, and we experience them even today. Time after time we see ourselves as wiser, smarter, or otherwise better equipped to know what is best for our lives. Even though we sometimes get it right, the reality is that time after time we mess it up. Still, we wrestle on. We are a determined lot, if nothing else.

But God wrestles in weakness and takes his licks too. In Genesis 3:15, God acknowledged that Satan would bruise someone's heel while having his own head crushed. Still, with this first broadside, Satan thought he had won the war, but the war was far from over. By the time Jesus died on the cross centuries later, Satan thought he'd won with the crushing, war-ending victory.

Physical death was the bruising of Jesus's heel. His resurrection was the ultimate wrestling move that crushed and destroyed Satan's power. Yes, Satan was decapitated that day, but he still threshes about like a suddenly beheaded snake. As he convulses about, we get hit by his stinging serpent's tail. As a result, we struggle, fight, and wrestle. Sometimes with each other. Often with ourselves. Almost always with God.

It breaks my heart to look back at all the struggles and heartaches I have suffered in my life. What makes it even worse is the realization that I brought on most of them. I made bad decisions and questionable calls. I said what I knew I shouldn't and went where I knew it would hurt me.

Need I say more? Yes, some of our hurts happen because we live in a broken sinful world. I get that. You get it too. But most of the time by far, my difficulties are self-inflicted or the long-term consequences of foolish mistakes in my past.

Wrestling with God? Yes, I wrestle for understanding, but mostly my wrestling is with my sinful nature. It is in direct conflict with the nature of God. So where does the weakness of God come in? He is all-powerful. He could fix all my brokenness in a heartbeat. With his mighty strength he could overpower all my willfulness. He could destroy in an instant all my selfishness. He could wipe out in a moment every evil desire that courses through my mind. But, that would take away my choice, and above all else, God wants me to choose him of my own volition.

So instead of exerting his mighty strength, he fights with one hand tied behind his back. He wields the weapons of foolishness and weakness. Maybe Paul says it best in 1 Corinthians when he talks about the foolishness of the cross being the power of God. In our human wisdom, we are inclined to see the crucifixion of Jesus as utter nonsense. But what we call the foolishness of God, Paul says "is wiser than human wisdom, and the weakness of God is stronger than human strength" (1:18–25). What is foolishness and weakness to the world is the power and strength of the cross!

Here's another way to see the weakness of God: He loves you! He loves me! That love compelled the sacrifice of Jesus. That love compelled the horror of the cross. As Jesus hung there, God was throwing his arms wide open to all who would come. Despite our failures, fears, insecurities, and doubts, God has wrestled with us and God has won. When I was a young boy, I liked to wrestle with my dad. Inevitably, he'd get me in a headlock and the only way out was to call calf-rope, to cry Uncle, or otherwise give up. As tough as Dad was, as tough as any other wrestling match might be, the hardest battle you will ever fight, the most difficult wrestling match you will ever endure, is surrendering your life to God. He wrestles in weakness because he is so strong.

Remember when the angels told Abraham that he and Sarah would have a son in their old age? Sarah, eavesdropping from her tent, laughed at the outrageous idea. She was, after all, ninety years old. Then the angel uttered a line that we all need to remember, now and forever: "Is anything too hard for the LORD?" (Gen. 18:14). You need to remember this for all the matches you've already endured, for all the struggles you still want answers for, and for all the times of wrestling that are yet to come.

Is there anything impossible for the Lord? No, not in this life or the life to come. In the meantime, until you have wrestled with God, you'll not know the depth of his love, the power of his hand, or the mercy and grace of his heart.

Say Uncle. Call calf-rope. Give up. Surrender to the One who changes everything.

GOING DEEPER

Read Genesis 3:8–15, 18:10–14, 32:24–30; 1 Corinthians 1:18–25

1. Why do you think Adam and Eve chose to disobey God? How did Satan go about deceiving them?

2. Have you ever yielded to deception because you wanted to? Could you say that was partly the problem with the sin of Adam and Eve?

3. How much pride do you place in your own abilities? Where do you see yourself as weak?

4. What do you feel powerless to change?

5. What is it that you wrestle with God over? Where or what do you need to surrender?

6. How does the cross show us God's weakness? How does the cross show us God's willingness to win?

Chapter 26

THE WEAKNESS OF GOD, PART TWO

Therefore, since we have been justified through faith, we have peace with God through our Lord Jesus Christ, through whom we have gained access by faith into this grace in which we now stand. And we boast in the hope of the glory of God. Not only so, but we also glory in our sufferings, because we know that suffering produces perseverance; perseverance, character; and character, hope. —Romans 5:1–4

My personal road back from tragedy, loss, and despair had any number of fitful starts and stops. Everybody processes in different ways and at different speeds. Some days I couldn't see my hand in front of my face. Those were hard, difficult times. Other days I could see far off in the distance. Those were emotional moments of hope where new recognition, new understanding, suddenly became clear. I celebrated those moments. They were painfully rare for a while, though. More days than not, I was exhausted by the process of discernment. I was an emotional basket case as I tried to sort through all the conflicting emotions and advice.

Have you ever run out of windshield washing solution? With a muddy windshield and no fluid, the wipers just make a smeared mess. Trying to see through that is disconcerting at best. At worst, it is exhausting. A quick trip to the corner store under those conditions is one thing. Trying to get through life with blurred muddy vision is entirely something else.

Many of us live in a state of perpetual confusion. Back in 1972, Johnny Nash had a hit song—"I Can See Clearly Now." I was ten years old. The world was bright; life was shiny and new. When I sang along with him, I had no idea what this existence would bring. I had no concept of days that would be dark and dreary. I couldn't imagine not being able to see clearly.

And then it happened. It doesn't matter how or why. Sometimes it is tragedy. Sometimes it is heartache, pain, and loss. Those things will obviously cloud up the windshield. But even without the big-ticket items like death, disease, and despair, life has a way of making it hard to see which way you are going. Right now, at this very moment of writing, my right eye is twitching, twitching, twitching. Google tells me it is caused by too much caffeine, fatigue, not enough sleep, or too much screen-time.

These days I'd opt for not enough sleep. The demands of family, ministry, and community keep life extraordinarily busy. Sometimes the busy is more than I can handle. Priorities get skewed and sometimes even dropped altogether. That leads to feeling like a failure, which in turn causes guilt, regret, and even more lack of sleep when I try to overcorrect.

Without much effort at all, most of us can create some vicious cycles of entrapment and enslavement. The more we try to get it right, the more out of balance our lives become. This should sound familiar to most of us unless you are living in denial. And you know the old saying: Denial is not a river in Egypt. Instead of a life-affirming watercourse, denial is more like a barren desert without any real and lasting hope.

I want to help people. I want to serve the spiritual, emotional, and even physical needs of the people around me. I want to help you. But that is hard to do when my tank is empty and my spiritual life is dry. The truth is quite simple. I long for the day when my windshield fluid reservoir is always full. When my wipers work as advertised. When my windshield is showroom-clean and clear.

In the meantime, I squint, sometimes fuss, and struggle to find a way to see through the mess. That is my world. While I squint and fuss, I also worry and stress. I am afraid of veering into the ditch or crossing the median. I am afraid of missing my exit or forgetting to turn. I am afraid of getting stuck in traffic or getting lost. All the while, my windshield is smeared, and I have nothing to clean it with. At least, it seems that way at times.

Problems compounded by problems. It's a conundrum for sure. Jesus tells us in Matthew 6:25–27 that we shouldn't worry, yet we still focus and obsess about all the necessities of life. We worry about food, clothing, paying the bills, and so on. And it's not that those things are somehow unimportant or that we shouldn't be good stewards and take care of business. But somehow in the process of living our lives, we forget how much God is in control of this world. And I know that.

Better yet, I want to believe that. Intellectually, I do. I know God is in charge. I am aware that this is his world. I don't know how many times I need to say it to convince us both, but I do. I also know I can do very little if anything about tomorrow. Unfortunately, as badly as I am messing up today, tomorrow doesn't seem to have much of a chance.

Why is this important to you? Because I am a stubborn old coot and refuse to believe I am alone. You're in this with me, like it or not. Even when the fears are unrealized, they are still there. Even when the worry is nothing but borrowed trouble, it is still there. Tragedy, heartache, and grief, however they make their appearance, will always smear your windshield. Life in the form of unrealized expectations, fears, and worries will always smudge your windshield. And then there is sin. Let me say from the outset, there is no dirty windshield like the one besmirched by sin.

And so, Paul reminds us that "all have sinned and fall short of the glory of God" (Rom. 3:23). He further tells us that in our sin, we have earned death, separation, from God (6:23). What does that look like? Look around you. The big-ticket hurts mentioned earlier—death, disease, despair—are all consequences of a windshield smeared by sin. No windshield cleaning fluid or the most technologically advanced windshield wipers are going to get that off. No sir, not a chance. Sin always leaves a mark. Always. Sin always leaves some sticky, nasty, bug-infested residue. The more we sully our windshield, the more wrecks and devastation we incur.

Let me affirm: life is beautiful, and I am thankful for it. But still, darkness has a way of creeping in.

Death, disease, despair? Nobody is immune.

A topsy-turvy life? It happens to us all.

The ravages of sin? The consequences are all around us.

That's where weakness comes in again. In 2 Corinthians 12, Paul longs for relief. Much ink has flowed in an attempt to unmask the exact nature of Paul's affliction. In verse 7, he calls it "a thorn in my flesh, a messenger of Satan, to torment me."

Some have thought this was a physical infirmity—bad eyesight, poor speaking ability. Others have suggested this was some sin temptation. And maybe it was. Paul would not be the first nor the last to beg God to remove some carnal desire's influence.

Still others have thought Paul's problem was relational. And why couldn't it have been? Sometimes craziness, stress, and chaos are the result of stressful, crazy, chaotic people inhabiting our lives. Problem people come in all shapes and sizes.

I don't have to have a definitive answer. I'd like to, but I don't. Whatever his affliction, it sounds painful, frustrating, and debilitating. And, as I live my life with its ups and downs, heartaches and struggles, and ever-present temptations, I am more focused than ever on God's message to Paul: "My grace is sufficient for you, for my power is made perfect in weakness" (2 Cor. 12:9).

If God is not going to take it all away now, I am thankful for the next best thing. Hallelujah for grace!

Grace in the moment. That's the answer for life when it goes psycho. God is ever-present!

Grace in the affliction. That's the answer for death, disease, and despair. However it comes, wherever it takes you, God is still there!

Grace in our sin. Don't give in. Don't give up. The blood of Jesus still cleanses, still saves. God still offers reconciliation!

God has told us his weakness is stronger than our strength. In our weakness, God's strength stands strong. "I lift up my eyes to the mountains—where does my help come from? My help comes from the LORD, the Maker of heaven and earth" (Ps. 121:1–2).

This is the end. All that is left to read in this book is the conclusion and epilogue. Chances are, if you are still breathing, you are in one of those muddy, smeared windshield situations.

Darkness has descended and despair has taken root.

Life is out of control and you feel quite powerless to turn it around.

Sin is having its way and temptations are exploding around you.

There are just as many chances your windshield is dirty even now from all three sources, even all three at once.

Been there; done that. Wearing the T-shirts even now.

It's not hopeless.

It's not over.

Come home to Jesus!

Come home to grace!

GOING DEEPER

Read Romans 5:1–11; Matthew 6:25–34; 2 Corinthians 12:1–10

1. Define reconciliation. Where is reconciliation missing in your life? What avenues do you need to take to find reconciliation?

2. What worries or fears plague you? Are some of those crippling you? How do you need to answer those concerns or put them in the right perspective?

3. Are there any chronic issues in your life? How are you handling them? Have you given up on God?

4. What does it mean for God to say, "My grace is sufficient"?

5. Where or how do you need to relax and trust God?

A TOGETHER ENDEAVOR

Then the LORD said to Cain, "Where is your brother Abel?"
"I don't know," he replied. "Am I my brother's keeper?"
—Genesis 4:9

Sometimes it seems I spend more time saying, "I am sorry," or, "I am wrong," than I do saying anything else. I am wrong a lot these days.

Wrong attitude.

Wrong heart.

Wrong actions.

Wrong words.

Wrong reasoning.

Wrong understanding.

I guess I should stop there. I could list wrongs all day long.

Being wrong is not fun, but being wrong is also an opportunity to grow into being right. I am, like you, a work in progress. Not necessarily a piece of fine art, but a piece of work? Yes, I have been called that before.

Once, I got my knickers all in a twist when I allowed politics, media, and plain old hard-headedness to get in my way of seeing some common sense truth. I also reverted to my inner

215

twelve-year-old boy. That's the boy who wasn't (isn't) going to let anybody tell him anything.

Here's what happened: I heard a prominent politician state for the first time what has now become a sort of truism: "It takes a village to raise a child." My biases showed up immediately. I blustered, disputed, and otherwise acted like the village idiot from an entirely different village. But there was truth in the saying. Lots of truth. Needed truth. But I refused to hear it. I was wrong. Should I say it again? I was wrong.

I understand the role of parents. I get that our children are primarily our responsibility. But I also understand the value and role of the community in the upbringing of our kids. I cannot effectively do it by myself. I need help. I need your help.

I need your help when my emotions get in the way of understanding what my children are trying to tell me. I need your help when my fears are overwhelming common sense and the normal course of life. I need your help when I cannot connect with one of my kids, but you can.

I need your help when your eyes see what mine do not. I need your help when my heart is in the wrong place and I am too prideful to see it. It does take a village, and I need you to be a part of mine. Better yet, I need to be deeply ensconced in yours. We need to share the same zip code.

Why do I need you in my life? Well, let me count the ways. I am sure you know the old saying, "If you want something done right, do it yourself." I tend to live my life like that. I tend to think that I must do it myself. I tend to feel like I am the only one who can. Worse, sometimes my attitude isn't what it should be (surprise, surprise), and I think I am the only one who will do whatever needs doing!

So there's that. And then, can you believe there's more? I often don't take care of myself as I should. I don't eat right. I don't get enough rest. I have disabled my off button and generally don't stop until I crash. Even when I don't crash, I still tend to deny there is a problem. Don't put me on a pedestal. Not this guy. I struggle with my demons, and we haven't begun to talk about spiritual struggles.

Can you handle a preacher who tells you the truth? Sometimes I get mad at God. Often the only time it seems I really talk with him is when I need something. These days I need something all the time. Boy howdy, my pride gets in the way too. And that might be the biggest issue of all. I don't really want a village to help me. I don't want to acknowledge my limitations. I don't want to acknowledge my needs. I don't want you to see me as needy, dependent, or weak.

For years, my life has been about me. Sure, I have a wife, kids, and ministry to do. But still, it's all about me until it isn't. Until I can't fake it or pretend or lie to myself or others anymore. Even salvation gets into the mix. I tend to make God's work in my life more about me than about him. And when the apostle Paul tells me to work out my own salvation with fear and trembling? That's me. All me. All by myself. All alone.

I am the rugged individualist. Strong. Isolated. Secure in myself. I am the guy. I can handle it. I am the example of what it looks like to be a Christian. Who needs a village? Not this guy! Except I do. I need you. I need you to be your brother's keeper. With tears streaming down my face, I need you. I need you even when I say I don't!

In Philippians 2:3–4, we are told to "do nothing out of selfish ambition or vain conceit. Rather, in humility value others above yourselves, not looking to your own interests but each of you to the interests of the others." Heaven help me! Those two-short, sweet, simple verses are the exact opposite of how I am inclined to live my life. Haven't you heard? We are supposed to look out for ourselves.

We need to brag occasionally, and toot our own horns to get the desired attention. Life is about me, right?

But that's not what Paul is telling us. Paul is saying life is about the other guy. Paul is reminding us that since life isn't about us, we need to quit being selfish—and that means taking care of one another. And then in the very next verse, he completely cuts our legs out from under us. Here's how you deal with people—here's how you treat others—here's how you remember your place: "In your relationships with one another, have the same mindset as Christ Jesus" (Phil. 2:5).

He went there, didn't he? Yes, he invoked Jesus, the One who did not seek equality with God—the One who came in the guise of a servant—the One who humbled himself enough to die on a cross.

That description of Jesus is completely foreign to the culture of our world. To the contrary, we demand equality, service, power, and obedience. That's what we expect from others. But in a dog-eat-dog world, the Jesus-way is different. A life that embraces the cross is not about self-preservation.

If you are like me, you may need a constant reminder to not be selfish. The Christian life is not the work of a rugged, isolated individualist. It is a "together endeavor." The life well-lived is best experienced and understood in the company of others. Nothing drives people away more than unrestrained selfishness. How I wish I had understood that before. How I wish I had known how badly I need you. When Paul asked God to remove his thorn in the flesh, he was acknowledging his need for God's mercy and grace too. He needed God's help. So do I. So do you. God's help is often available through the strength of others.

Life is full of lessons. Some of them are extremely hard to learn. In my pride, anger, resentment, bitterness, pain, and grief, I retreated into my shell like a turtle. It was a tough, tight shell. There was no room inside for anyone else.

In pride, I became a pusher. My drug of choice was isolation. If it was possible to push someone away, I pushed with all my might. I rejected folks who wanted to help me. I hurt feelings. I turned my back on the work of God through others in my life. That, to date, has been my greatest failure—my biggest flaw.

We need each other, and the only way we are going to shine like stars is together. I need your light. You need mine. And, as it turns out, the answer to Cain's question is yes. I am my brother's keeper. You are your sister's minder. And while we focus on the murder of Abel as Cain's great sin, it might have never happened had Cain not become selfish and isolated.

Whatever your story might be, whatever struggle, pain, and anguish you wrestle with, you are only alone if you choose to be. So don't. Don't be alone. Let others in. Let others help. Quit being stubborn and prideful (which is often only another way to define selfishness). Recognize your need. Embrace those who care. Receive hugs. Give hugs.

At the beginning of this book, I said there needed to be a twelve-step program for people like me. And there is. That same group is available to you. Since you are reading this particular book, there's a good chance that you already belong. In fact, you are probably a regular attendee at the meetings.

If you are still scratching your head and wondering, your twelve-step group is a church. If you don't belong to a church, find one. Find one now. If you are already involved, learn how to be more honest about your struggles. Tell someone your hurts. Quit hiding your failings. Life is too short and precious to wallow alone.

I could use a hug.

How about you?

EPILOGUE

At the double funeral for Karen and Cole, a video montage of family pictures was shown. Jeremy Camp's song "There Will Be a Day" accompanied the video. All these years later, I still cannot listen to that song without experiencing cloudy vision. As I write this last little bit by hand, I am hoping Katie, my administrative assistant, can read through the water spots on the page to type my words. But, as the tears flow, I am smiling too.

Some of the tears are sad—for all the loss, all the pain. Not just my own, but that of my children—for the whole big family of parents, in-laws, siblings, aunts, uncles, cousins, and friends. We cannot forget all the friends who suffered too. But some of the tears are happy tears for all that God has done—for all that God continues to do. Though smiling and laughing at memories happens often, fresh tears are never far away.

Yes, there will be a day when all the broken is broken no more, when all the wrongs are righted, when pain is no longer even a memory. But while we wait for that day, while we long for the ultimate healing, open your eyes to the ever-present grace of God. There is still great beauty in this world to be found. There is still much joy to be had. Life is still worth living.

So keep wrestling.

Don't quit.

Remember this is just a battle—God has already won the war.

Don't miss out on the day you can have now—and the day that is coming tomorrow.

May God bless us all!